Converting the Imagination

HORIZONS *IN* RELIGIOUS EDUCATION is a book series sponsored by the Religious Education Association: An Association of Professors, Practitioners and Researchers in Religious Education. It was established to promote new scholarship and exploration in the academic field of Religious Education. The series will include both seasoned educators and newer scholars and practitioners just establishing their academic writing careers.

Books in this series reflect religious and cultural diversity, educational practice, living faith, and the common good of all people. They are chosen on the basis of their contributions to the vitality of religious education around the globe. Writers in this series hold deep commitments to their own faith traditions, yet their work sets forth claims that might also serve other religious communities, strengthen academic insight, and connect the pedagogies of religious education to the best scholarship of numerous cognate fields.

The posture of the Religious Education Association has always been ecumenical and multi-religious, attuned to global contexts, and committed to affecting public life. These values are grounded in the very institutions, congregations, and communities that transmit religious faith. The association draws upon the interdisciplinary richness of religious education connecting theological, spiritual, religious, social science and cultural research and wisdom. Horizons of Religious Education aims to heighten understanding and appreciation of the depth of scholarship resident within the discipline of religious education, as well as the ways it impacts our common life in a fragile world. Without a doubt, we are inspired by the wonder of teaching and the awe that must be taught.

Jack L. Seymour (co-chair), Garrett-Evangelical Theological Seminary

Dean G. Blevins (co-chair), Nazarene Theological Seminary

Elizabeth Caldwell (co-chair), McCormick Theological Seminary

Dori Grinenko Baker, The Fund for Theological Education & Sweet Briar College

Sondra H. Matthaei, Saint Paul School of Theology

Siebren Miedema, Vrije Universiteit Amsterdam

Hosffman Ospino, Boston College

Mai-Anh Le Tran, Eden Theological Seminary

Anne Streaty Wimberly, Interdenominational Theological Seminary

Converting the Imagination

Teaching to Recover Jesus' Vision for Fullness of Life

PATRICK R. MANNING

PICKWICK *Publications* · Eugene, Oregon

CONVERTING THE IMAGINATION
Teaching to Recover Jesus' Vision for Fullness of Life

Horizons in Religious Education Series

Copyright © 2020 Patrick R. Manning. All rights reserved. Except for brief quotations in critical publications or reviews, no part of this book may be reproduced in any manner without prior written permission from the publisher. Write: Permissions, Wipf and Stock Publishers, 199 W. 8th Ave., Suite 3, Eugene, OR 97401.

Pickwick Publications
An Imprint of Wipf and Stock Publishers
199 W. 8th Ave., Suite 3
Eugene, OR 97401

www.wipfandstock.com

PAPERBACK ISBN: 978-1-7252-6053-5
HARDCOVER ISBN: 978-1-7252-6052-8
EBOOK ISBN: 978-1-7252-6054-2

Cataloguing-in-Publication data:

Names: Manning, Patrick R., author.

Title: Converting the imagination : teaching to recover Jesus' vision for fullness of life / Patrick R. Manning.

Description: Eugene, OR: Pickwick Publications, 2020. | Horizons in Religious Education Series | Includes bibliographical references.

Identifiers: ISBN 978-1-7252-6053-5 (paperback) | ISBN 978-1-7252-6052-8 (hardcover) | ISBN 978-1-7252-6054-2 (ebook)

Subjects: LCSH: Imagination—Religious aspects—Christianity. | Religious education.

Classification: BR115.16 M36 2020 (print) | BR115.16 (ebook)

Manufactured in the U.S.A.   05/13/20

For my children, Emily and Luca,
who have given me new eyes with which to see the world.

"Where there is no vision, the people perish."

—Proverbs 29:18

"For the glory of God is the human being fully alive,
and the true life of humanity is the vision of God."

—Irenaeus of Lyons

CONTENTS

EDITORS' PREFACE

As we seek to make sense of our worlds, we draw on the knowledge and perspectives that have been taught by our elders, peers, communities, and cultures. Moreover, the images that surround us focus what we see and how we feel and live. If that knowledge and set of images are rich and nuanced, a person's view of the world is expansive. If the perspectives learned are narrow and closed, the views of people tend to be closed and anxious. Dr. Patrick R. Manning of Seton Hall University in South Orange, New Jersey, the oldest Roman Catholic diocesan university in the United States, engages the current narrowing of the power of religious imagination to enrich our personal and public lives. In this sixth book in the *HORIZONS in RELIGIOUS EDUCATION* series of the Religious Education Association, he describes the current disintegration of religious imagination and the concomitant decline in the power of religious communities to help people develop a coherent worldview. Instead a cacophony of images of consumption and competition fill the Western world. Addressing this crisis of meaning, he offers ways to help people re-engage religious faith and living.

Drawing on his experiences in higher education and in parish life, he shows why many, particularly the young, have become anxious and adrift. They have been blinded to the riches of the religious traditions. They, therefore, are missing the wealth of meanings provided by these religious communities: perspectives about living ethically, about engaging each other respectfully, about connecting deeply with our spirits, and about working together to create a world of value.

Dr. Manning grounds his work in theological reflection about the life and message of Jesus as well as in an analysis of contemporary psychology and cognitive science. He demonstrates the ways religious imagination can be formed and enhanced. He shows how a coherent worldview can be shaped to affect public life. Furthermore, he provides a method of teaching to enrich the religious imagination that has been tested in both parish and school settings. That threefold method includes (1) stimulating the imagination, (2) expanding the imagination, and (3) embracing a new way of imagining. He invites us to "see anew"—to see how we can build communities so that all may thrive.

While his vision is clearly Christian, Dr. Manning has offered us a method of teaching that can be considered by other religious communities. He is touching how all communities of meaning transfer visions from one generation to the next. Visions come to live in others as imaginations are broadened with the richest resources of our various human communities. We live in a diverse world. We find ways to live together and to build a world when we share the best of ourselves and our resources. Dr. Manning provides concrete tools for enlivening dialogues and meaning and enriching our imaginations with the power and value of religious faith. We invite you to read this book, try its tools in your classes, share it with friends in your faith community, and begin conversations to enrich our common life.

—Jack L. Seymour, Professor Emeritus, Garrett-Evangelical Theological Seminary, Evanston, Illinois, USA. Co-chair, Horizons Editorial Board.

—Hosffman Ospino, Boston College, Boston, Massachusetts, USA. Co-chair, Horizons Editorial Board.

—Mai-Anh Le Tran, Garrett-Evangelical Theological Seminary, Evanston, Illinois, USA. Co-chair, Horizons Editorial Board.

GRATITUDES

I have poured much of myself into this book, and I have been able to do so only insofar as I have drawn deeply upon the well of my community. Although I identify just a few people by name here, I acknowledge that this project has been shaped in various ways by the countless friends, family, colleagues, and models who have influenced me. First of all, I want to thank Jack Seymour for his encouragement with this project in its early stages and for faithfully guiding it to completion. I offer my profuse thanks to Bud Horell for his careful reading of multiple versions of this manuscript and for his keen questions, insights, and suggestions. This book is far stronger than it would have been otherwise on account of the feedback I received from these two senior scholars. I am grateful to Ulrich Guthrie for her expert editorial touch as well as for her helpful challenges. Thanks also to Max Engel, Fr. Kevin Sandberg, Paul Mitchell, and Cindy Cameron, who offered feedback on early forms or parts of the book. And finally I reserve my most heartfelt thanks for my wife, Margaret, for her constant love and support. It is hard for me to imagine this book (or much of anything in my life) coming to fruition without her.

A FADING VISION

"I came that they may have life, and have it abundantly" (John 10:10, NRSV). Jesus' promise clearly enticed people in his day, so much so that some of them dropped whatever they were doing to "come and see" what this abundance of life might entail (John 1:39, NRSV). Does Jesus' vision of the fullness of life exert the same attractive power today?

It did for me. In fact, I remember a very particular moment in my life when this vision snapped into focus. It came one evening toward the end of my final year at college when I was gathered in the chapel of my dormitory with fellow residents and friends to celebrate the weekly 10 p.m. Sunday Mass. Every chair was filled, and people sat along the back wall and on the floor around the altar. The presider, the rector of our residence hall, was concluding the Eucharistic prayer, his words heavy with meaning. He looked around the chapel, catching the eyes of those gathered, with a solemn expression that said we are doing something important here, something in which we are fortunate to participate. His words gave way to the reverberating sound of the piano, guitar, and dozens of voices filling the room with a resounding hymn. My heart, too, felt full as I stepped forward to distribute Communion to my friends. Some weeks before I had been accepted into a service-through-teaching program that would take me to a Catholic high school in Tennessee for the next two years. As I pressed the Body of Christ into the outstretched palms of my friends, I thought to myself, "This is what teaching is: bringing Christ and the fullness of life he offers to others. This is what my life will be about."

In many ways, this moment encapsulated the life of abundance that I had been gradually living into for much of my life up to that point and in a particularly intense way for the previous four years. During that time,

I had lived, studied, and worshipped within a university community that expressed the fecundity of the Christian imagination in its architecture, its scholarship, and, most importantly, in the interactions among its members. I had studied the Great Books and the Christian theological tradition and found better answers to my questions than I had hitherto discovered. More importantly, I learned to ask better questions than I had previously formulated. Of greatest consequence was befriending people who were truly alive, who celebrated the joys of life—food, music, conversation—with the relish of a child sinking her toes into the grainy warmth of a sandy beach. These were people whose eyes shone brightly when they interrogated life's big questions and shared their dreams of how they might give their gift to the world.

Knowing such people helped me to see and feel the meaningfulness of the Christian conviction that we are all children of God. Overwhelmed with gratitude for the abundance of blessings in my life, I increasingly came to see life as a gift and the world as originating from love and returning to love. This world made sense to me, and I was confident of my role in it. My life was not perfect, but it was good and it was full. Jesus' promise seemed true.

Soon thereafter I graduated. In the years that followed, my vision of life was tested by adversity, heartbreak, and loss. I moved from my Midwestern, Catholic university community, where I felt very much at home, to a new school community in Memphis, Tennessee, constituted by predominantly Baptist, African-American colleagues, and students whose culture was very different from that which I had known. I shared in the grief of students who had witnessed the violent murder of family members. Around the same time, relationships that had been central in my life were breaking down. All of this complicated my vision of the life of abundance to which Jesus calls us, but it did not destroy it. Only years later, as I reflected back on this period of my life with the benefit of insights from research and study, could I appreciate why that vision held and why that of others faced with similar challenges did not.

These days I occupy the other side of the classroom as a college professor. True to my original vision, I teach and write with the aim of inviting others into the fullness of life that I have discovered in following after Jesus. This is the aim that motivated me to write this book. In recent years, this goal has come to look increasingly ambitious, for I have found that the experience of most of my students is very different from my own.

One class I teach for first-year students, a required core course centered around the big questions and classic texts of the Catholic intellectual tradition, has been particularly revealing in this regard. At this stage in their lives, these students are full of excitement and nervousness about college, new relationships, and their future. With the world opening up before them, they are growing in awareness of the perennial challenges of being human and the pressing issues of our day. They are beginning to sort out where they fit in the world and to assert themselves as agents of social change. It is exhilarating to witness the reaction when the students' raw energy comes into contact with the great questions and texts of the Christian tradition.

These students are different from recent generations of students in several ways. For one thing, they tend to be more respectful of a diversity of perspectives and slower to judge or criticize beliefs that differ from their own. At the same time, they are less willing to accept tradition and authority for its own sake. That past generations believed something to be important or that church officials proclaim a doctrine to be true is for them not sufficient reason to accept it for themselves. They seek verification in their own lives and the lives of their contemporaries. Like every generation, they seek meaning and fullness for their lives. However, I find that their search for meaning has a different flavor. There seems to be a greater sense of urgency—even desperation—perhaps because they are less inclined to take for granted the traditions and beliefs of their forbearers and so have little foundation upon which to build. Often their search for meaning embarks not from the safe harbor of family religion but rather far out in the open waters of pluralistic, postmodern culture with the shore nowhere in sight. Even those who have grown up within a well-established religious tradition are less confident that it can provide real meaning for their lives. When these students arrive in the classroom, they bring these gifts, limitations, aspirations, and anxieties with them. Of course, there is the usual anxiousness that comes with being a young adult—anxiousness about making friends, earning good grades, getting a job—but what I have seen in my students in recent years goes beyond these perennial stressors.

Take David for example. When I met David, he had recently arrived on campus and was eager to begin the new adventure of college. He dived right in, meeting lots of people, joining clubs and sports teams, and taking full advantage of the weekend (and sometimes weekday) party scene. David is handsome, funny, and likeable. He comes from a family of considerable means and Catholic devotion. His father's success in the business world has radiated to David in the form of professional contacts, internships, and other forms of social capital. Suffice it to say that David's prospects for the future were bright.

Given all that I knew about David, it took me by surprise when late in the year he confided in me that he had been struggling with depression for several months. After a fast start to the academic year, he had settled into an unshakable malaise. His world had faded to grey. He lacked energy for things that had once been passions and experienced no joy or excitement in what should have been one of the most exciting periods of his life. He isolated himself from friends and neglected assignments. A broken relationship seems to have been the initial trigger, but there was more to it than that, he said. Despite his Catholic upbringing and enviable career prospects, he lacked a sense of purpose in his life. He just didn't see any point, any meaning to it all.

David's story is not unusual these days. My students frequently make comments to the effect that they feel anxious "like literally every single day," that "there is nothing to see . . . nothing to feel," that they "view the world as a threat" and "feel lost in the shuffle." From 2008 to 2017 there was a 71 percent increase in young adults experiencing serious psychological distress.[1] One in four young adults in this country has a diagnosable mental illness.[2] Generally speaking, college students are reporting the lowest levels of mental health in at least a quarter century.[3] Many readers of this book could undoubtedly name students or acquaintances of their own who struggle with mental health issues. The world of higher education is now coming to the realization that we have a full-blown mental health crisis on our hands. What we have been slower to grasp—and this is a central claim of this book—is the fact that *this mental health crisis is only one facet of a much larger crisis of meaning affecting much of the Western world.*

As a teacher, it pains me to hear a student say that he cannot find meaning in his life or that he is so ridden with anxiety that he cannot function normally. As a Christian educator, a situation like David's troubles me on another level because his Catholic faith appears not to be helping him. He could not be further away from the fullness of life Jesus promised, a life supposedly marked by wholeness, joy, meaning, and purpose. Of course,

1. Twenge et al., "Age, Period, and Cohort Trends."
2. NAMI, "Top Mental Health Challenges Facing College Students."
3. Lewin, "Record Level of Stress Found in College Freshmen."

being a Christian does not preclude suffering. Conditions like clinical depression often have a genetic basis that no amount of religion can fix. Besides, Jesus virtually guaranteed that suffering awaits those who follow him.[4] Nonetheless, Christian faith is supposed to be a source of hope in moments of difficulty, a life raft for life's shipwrecks. Like many of his contemporaries, David found none of the above in the faith he inherited from his parents.[5] The homilies he had heard on a weekly basis in church and the religious teachings he had learned over years of Catholic education seemed insubstantial to the point of irrelevance in the face of his very concrete, very real existential struggles. Listening as he poured out his bleeding heart, I could not help but feel that we as a church had failed this young man. It is my hope that this book will facilitate a conversation among Christian educators about how we can do better.

THE DEEP ROOTS OF DISAFFILIATION AND MENTAL DECLINE

David's situation is in a way paradigmatic of an ever-growing group of contemporary Christians. I speak of them as a group in a loose sense, for on the surface they may look very different from one another. They are not only college-aged people like David but also adolescents and mature adults. Some may attend worship services every week, others a couple of times a year, others never. Some may have even abandoned their church for a new denomination, a new set of spiritual practices, or nothing at all. What they all have in common is a Christian heritage that has lost its vital meaning for their lives. When they were searching for meaning in the midst of a breakup, the death of a loved one, or simply the day-to-day, they found nothing in their Christian faith to help them.

Of this group it is those who no longer identify with any religion—the so-called "nones"—who garner the most attention. This attention is due in part to their rapidly growing numbers. As of 2019, 26 percent of the adult US population identified as religiously unaffiliated, up 9 percent since only ten years before.[6] For millennials, the figure is more than 40 percent.[7] The Catholic Church has been particularly hard hit by disaffiliation with

4. See Mark 8:34; Matt 10:22.

5. See McCarty and Vitek, *Going, Going, Gone*, 14.

6. Pew Research Center, "In US, Decline of Christianity Continues at Rapid Pace."

7. Pew Research Center, "In US, Decline of Christianity Continues at Rapid Pace."

nearly 13 percent of all Americans now describing themselves as "former Catholics."[8] There exists a great diversity of beliefs and practices among the nones, a fact that journalists and authors sometimes overlook in their reports. For example, a significant number of people who select "none" on surveys attend worship services, and far more consider religion important to their lives.[9] Although they no longer desire to bind themselves to the religious institutions of their ancestors, many persist in a spiritual quest for meaning, value, and transcendence.

Despite outward appearances, many people who retain their traditional religious affiliation are not so different from those who abandoned theirs. There are many who continue to call themselves "Christian" in whose lives religion and spirituality factor much less than in those of some nones. This seems to be the case for a growing number of Catholics, who have in many ways absorbed a secular outlook[10] and who in the past half century have grown virtually indistinguishable from non-Christians in their moral views.[11] For them, the vestiges of Christianity may remain, but their faith plays little role in shaping their decisions and actions and they maintain little in the way of a personal relationship with God. As Ronald Rolheiser puts it, they profess belief in God, but "rarely is there a vital sense of God within the bread and butter of life."[12] Many of the disaffiliated experience the same hangover or nostalgia for religion.[13] They may even be more proactive than their "religious" counterparts in seeking the transcendent, although they may seek it in nature or meditation or CrossFit rather than in an institutional religion.

This phenomenon is not unique to Catholicism. Recent surveys show a huge drop in the number of Mainline Protestants who feel certain of God's existence.[14] We see similar trends in other religious groups.[15] One-in-five Jews now describe themselves as having no religion, with millennial Jews being far more likely to identify in this way.[16] The number of American

---

8. Pew Research Center, "America's Changing Religious Landscape."

9. Pew Research Center, "Nones on the Rise."

10. Cf. Synod of Bishops, "New Evangelization," no. 6.

11. O'Toole, *Faithful*, 302–4.

12. Rolheiser, *Shattered Lantern*, 17.

13. See Ozment, *Grace Without God*.

14. Pew Research Center, "US Public Becoming Less Religious."

15. Muslims are a different case, however. See Lipka, "Muslims and Islam."

16. Pew Research Center, "Portrait of Jewish Americans."

Hindus who consider religion very important to them has been cut almost in half in the past decade.[17] While there are numerous examples of movements of young people recommitting to their faith as many of their peers are heading for the exits, the general direction of the trend is clear.[18] The above statistics suggest that religious disaffiliation is a widespread phenomenon and that whatever is causing people to abandon their religion transcends the particularities of any one religious community.

Although the recent exodus from organized religion in the United States is certainly cause for concern, that is not the issue I want to address in this book; rather, it is only part of the issue. There seems to be a deeper problem affecting not only the "nones" but also many people who still identify as religious. On one level, these individuals indicate that they are not finding meaning in the faith of their forebears. They say things like "it didn't quite make much sense to me" and "I don't think that being Catholic or [any] other type of religion will change my life."[19] But the issue appears to go even deeper than religion. Many contemporary persons are simply not finding meaning anywhere. In the words of one young person, they are "wounded by . . . existential anxiety" and "searching for the meaning of life."[20] *This lack of meaning and the existential distress it precipitates are the central issues I address in this book.* My concern is not only for millennials or the religiously unaffiliated but rather for all those people who are presently failing to find meaning for their lives in their religious tradition, particularly the Christian tradition.

No issue is more fundamental for religious educators. Religious education as I understand it is not merely about teaching information on religion. Insofar as it touches the religious dimension of the human person, it involves exploring questions of meaning, relationship, and transcendence. Especially when carried out as one of the constitutive elements within the life of a faith community, religious education contributes to the work of inviting the personal and communal transformation that leads to wholeness of life.[21] I trust that any religious educators who conceive of their work

17. Pew Research Center, "US Public Becoming Less Religious."

18. Colleen Carroll explores such a countermovement within Catholicism in her book *The New Faithful*. Acknowledging the significance of these countermovements within both Catholic and Protestant Christianity, I will focus my attention in this book on the general trend toward disaffiliation and its causes.

19. McCarty and Vitek, *Going, Going, Gone*, 23, 14.

20. Santiago, "Briana Santiago Synod Witness."

21. The term "religious education" contains numerous layers of meaning, which are

in similar terms will likewise consider it of paramount concern that people are failing to find meaning in religion and life in general.

That a problem exists is widely acknowledged, but the source of the problem is not well understood. One well-worn explanation is that modernization and the increase of human knowledge dispel the shadows of ignorance and superstition in which religion thrives, making its eventual disappearance inevitable.[22] Scholars have now generally rejected this linear account of secularization, as the relationship between modernization and religion has proven quite complicated. Charles Taylor is one prominent scholar to have criticized this account, what he calls the "subtraction story" of secularization.[23] Underpinning Taylor's critique is the psychological insight that people's deeply embedded worldviews are highly resistant to revision based on new information and rational argumentation alone.[24] Radical change in the way people make sense of reality does not occur primarily on the intellectual level but rather at the level of the preconscious operations of the imagination.

For communities and the individuals who live within those communities, it is images, stories, rituals, and practices rather than theory that most powerfully shape their intuitive understanding or sense of the way the world is. Taylor describes this way in which a community collectively and pre-theoretically imagines the world as a "cosmic imaginary."[25] For centuries, even those who were only marginally Christian viewed reality through the lens of a Christian imaginary. The accepted view was that the world they lived in had been created by God, that their successes and sufferings in life were influenced by spiritual forces, both good and evil, and that their eternal fate depended on living a good moral life. Because

evident in this work. On one level, religious education can refer to an interdisciplinary field of academic study that draws upon and dialogues with scholarship in other fields of study, including theology, religious studies, and education. This book is a work of religious education understood in this sense. However, within faith communities "religious education" more commonly refers to the efforts of the community to educate its members in faith (i.e., a near synonym for faith formation or catechesis). Although the boundary is somewhat permeable, it is important to clarify that in this book unless otherwise specified I usually intend the latter meaning when I use this term.

22. See, e.g., Durkheim, *Division of Labor in Society*; Marx, *Critique of Hegel's "Philosophy of Right"*; Weber, *Protestant Ethic and the Spirit of Capitalism*.

23. Taylor, *Secular Age*, 22.

24. Taylor's claim receives support from contemporary research in psychology (e.g., Haidt, *Righteous Mind*) and neuroscience (e.g., Sharot, *Influential Mind*).

25. Taylor, *Secular Age*, 323.

everyone took God's existence for granted, to think of a world devoid of God was literally unimaginable.

However, over the course of the past 500 years, religious, social, moral, and scientific developments contributed to the erosion of the Christian imaginary and the emergence of a myriad of visions of human flourishing, none of which have been able to provide the stable meaning previously afforded by the old Christian imaginary. Christians no longer live in a Christian world inhabited entirely by other Christians. Today they live in a world where the Big Bang rivals (in the minds of some) divine creation as an explanation for the genesis of the universe. Their neighbors are not all Christians like themselves but also Muslims and ethical culturists and atheists. Living in a cultural milieu marked by such a diversity of beliefs, it is much more difficult for anyone to take a particular view of reality (whether theistic, atheistic, or other) as a given. Increasingly, modern persons are forced to sort through the constellations of competing accounts of reality and cobble together for themselves a worldview that gives meaning and coherence to their lived experience.

Taylor's analysis suggests that, if so many people today are failing to cope mentally with life's challenges, that this is not only because the world has grown more fast-paced and complicated. Equally important is the fact that many contemporary persons lack a mental framework for making sense of it all.[26] When people lack the means of making meaning of life events, they are less able to handle the ordinary and extraordinary stressors of modern life (final exams, breakups, layoffs, economic recessions) and so succumb to mental illness.[27] Imperfect though it may have been,[28] the Christian imaginary provided such a framework for previous generations, but members of this generation are increasingly abandoning that framework on account of its perceived lack of relevance or meaningfulness and failing to find an adequate alternative.[29]

---

26. Taylor's theory is corroborated by the psychological research of Robert Kegan, which I will engage in greater depth in chapter 2.

27. See Frankl, *Man's Search for Meaning*; Antonovsky, *Unraveling the Mystery of Health*.

28. See Jennings, *Christian Imagination*; Pui-lan, *Postcolonial Imagination and Feminist Theology* for some critiques of how the Christian imagination has been distorted throughout history.

29. Numerous contemporary studies provide evidence of the salutary effect of religious/spiritual practices and culture on people's sense of coherence and well-being. See, e.g., Bowman and Small, "Exploring a Hidden Form of Minority Status"; Jeserich, "Can

IN SEARCH OF A RESPONSE

Taylor's analysis, corroborated by current research on how human beings make meaning and by what I see routinely in Catholic schools and parishes, has convinced me that underlying increasing disaffiliation and mental health issues is a widespread crisis of meaning. Other scholars have previously diagnosed this problem.[30] Although it is certainly worthwhile to deepen that analysis, my intent in this book is to make a contribution to the body of projects aimed at responding to the problem.[31]

While I wholeheartedly affirm proposals for addressing these issues by a variety of means, I believe that religious educators qua teachers have a crucial role to play. More specifically, I believe religious educators can train learners in formal educational settings in ways that will assist them in making sense of their lives—including their faith lives—amidst the fragmenting forces of postmodern culture. If people are not finding meaning in the Christian tradition, it is not because there is no meaning to be found. The problem lies with the failure of Christian communities to adapt to new cultural challenges to faith.

The problem is at root a problem of meaning, and meaning is always fundamentally a matter of the imagination. Nostalgic appeals to the old Christian imaginary will not help such people insofar as that imaginary will never again enjoy the unquestioned acceptance it once did. Nevertheless, what teachers of the faith can do to help contemporary Christians is train them in the habits of imagining that are necessary for constructing a meaningful Christian worldview in a pluralistic and rapidly evolving culture.

For a number of years now I have striven to do just that by taking a more imagination-centered approach in my teaching. On the one hand, I have made an effort to help students tap into the Christian tradition as a source of deep meaning flowing from Jesus' life-giving vision for the world. On the other hand, rather than viewing students' critical questions and desire for deeper meaning as a threat, I have endeavored to invite and develop these capacities through their engagement with the Christian tradition in the confidence that doing so would better prepare them to live meaningful, faithful lives in postmodern society. As I have refined this approach and

---

Sense of Coherence Be Modified by Religious/Spiritual Interventions?"

30. Astin et al., *Cultivating the Spirit*; Berger, *Sacred Canopy*; Doran, *Theology and the Dialectics of History*; Small, *Making Meaning*.

31. I will engage this body of research directly in chapter 3.

applied it with greater intentionality and consistency, I have noticed that my students are more attentive, interested, and engaged with the course than in previous years. I have had greater success tapping into their passion and creativity and have observed growth in their capacity for reflecting on their own meaning-making. As my students have imaginatively engaged the wisdom, symbols, and visions of Christianity (and other religious traditions), they have (re)discovered greater meaning for their lives and, in many cases, grown more hopeful and less anxious.

In the following pages, I lay out the specifics of the pedagogical approach that facilitated these transformations. Chapters 1 through 3 establish the groundwork for a pedagogy of transforming imaginations. I take as my point of departure in chapter 1 Jesus' timeless call to personal transformation (i.e., conversion). I argue that today, as in ages past, only by undergoing a radical transformation in our desiring, imagining, and living can human beings, who are divided within themselves by both external and internal forces, achieve wholeness.

In chapter 2, I draw upon contemporary research in cognitive science and cognitional theory to understand the unique challenges to faith and meaning-making confronting Christians today. Through this analysis, the picture comes into focus as to how new mental challenges in society, coupled with the erosion of traditional resources for making sense of life, have contributed to current trends toward religious disaffiliation and existential dis-integration. This research provides the basis for my hypothesis that reclaiming Christian faith as a way of life and an integrating meaning framework in the current context will require (among other things) at least a critical mass of Christians to grow into a "post-critical" form of religious consciousness, that is, a form of meaning-making that is self-aware, self-authoring, self-transcending, and that unites the powers of imaginative thinking and critical reasoning. The term "post-critical consciousness" will likely strike the average reader as somewhat esoteric, but in essence it is merely a psychologically informed way of describing the most recent development in the ongoing evolution of human spirituality. Chapter 3 relates this new development in religious consciousness to earlier manifestations of Christian interiority and explains how development to this new form of interiority occurs.

Building upon these foundational chapters, in chapters 4 through 6 I present a three-phase pedagogical process that has enabled me to help learners take possession of their imagining and recover meaning and wholeness in their lives. In presenting this new process, I am consciously appropriating and extending the examples and work of Jesus and other educators and scholars. Notable among these are Mary Warnock, Kathleen Fischer, and Richard Côte, three prophets of the imagination whose seminal works have drawn attention to the vital place of the imagination in human living, education, and faith.[32] In a sense, my own book is an effort to respond to their pleas for renewed attention to the imagination as have other religious educators like Maria Harris, Jerome Berryman, and Charles Foster.[33] Where Harris's and Foster's books focus more on the imagination of the teacher or the educating community, my focus in this book is on the imaginations of learners and helping learners cultivate ways of imagining that are more adequate to our present context. (Barryman's book is distinct in its focus on play.) In the final chapter of this book, in addition to offering some clarifications concerning my pedagogical approach, I will point to still more efforts by other religious educators, leaders, and spiritual guides that I see as complementing my own project and forming the basis for a comprehensive response to the current crisis of meaning.

I have developed this pedagogical approach by teaching in Catholic schools and parishes in the United States and through reflection primarily upon my own Catholic Christian tradition. I can therefore testify to its appropriateness for Christian (particularly Catholic) religious education in the United States context. Nonetheless, the issues I confront here—religious disaffiliation, the struggle to make meaning, communal and personal fragmentation—affect people of other faith communities as well, both in the United States and elsewhere. Insofar as religious educators from other traditions and contexts recognize their own challenges in those I describe here, I trust they will find something of benefit in what follows.

Dire as the situation is for many, the present is a moment of opportunity as well. Coming to grips with the fact that many Davids in our society and our faith communities are failing to make sense of their lives may turn out to be the impetus we need to rethink the ways we worship, build community, and hand on the faith. It may prompt us to look for new resources and ways of envisioning and living into the reign of God. Indeed, it may be that God is showing us a new way forward precisely in the questions, criticisms, and seeking of our young people and those who

---

32. Warnock, *Imagination*; Fischer, *Inner Rainbow*; Côte, *Lazarus! Come Out!*

33. Harris, *Teaching and Religious Imagination*; Barryman, *Godly Play*; Foster, *From Generation to Generation*, esp. chapter 5.

express dissatisfaction with our religious traditions as they encounter them. This may very well be a once-in-an-era opportunity to revitalize our faith communities by rediscovering resources within our faith traditions and within each other for responding to our deepest questions, concerns, and hopes and for serving the needs of the world.

chapter 1

JESUS' VISION FOR FULLNESS OF LIFE

The present is a moment of crisis for many individuals and faith communities. Many people experience their lives as overwhelming, fragmented, and bereft of meaning. Some causes of this existential distress are novel, and we will examine these in due time. However, there is nothing new about the search for a life of fullness and meaning. To be human is to seek meaning, and for two thousand years, people have found meaning for their lives in the Christian tradition. But now, for some reason, increasing numbers of people are no longer finding meaning there.

It is my purpose in this book to understand better why this has happened so as to help Christian communities address the challenges of postmodern culture more effectively. The problem is in large part a problem of making meaning. That being the case, it will be helpful to begin by examining the meaning Christianity has historically given to people's lives and how Jesus invites us into a life that is not merely meaningful but overflowing with an "abundance" of meaning (John 10:10, NRSV). Once we have a basic understanding of human meaning-making and Christian meaning, we will be better prepared to examine how meaning-making breaks down and how meaning—including religious meaning—can be lost.

LOVING AS JESUS LOVES

Jesus' teachings have the potential to speak to our human needs as powerfully today as they did when he first presented them to his first-century audience. Jesus understood his followers' fears and anxieties about the world they lived in, their livelihood, and what the future would bring, and he spoke words of peace to these concerns.[1] He also helped his followers to recognize that the greatest obstacles to fullness of life are internal rather than external. He told his disciples, "Do you not see that whatever goes into a person from outside cannot defile. . . . It is what comes out of a person that defiles. For it is from within, from the human heart, that evil intentions come" (Mark 7:18–21, NRSV).

Jesus knew that the heart is the key. For him and his Jewish contemporaries, the heart (*leb* in Hebrew, *kardia* in Greek) represented the center of the human person, the source of the human's intellectual powers as well as the emotions. Whatever we set our hearts upon will determine where our lives lead and who we become. Although our understanding of human anatomy is different today, Jesus' fundamental insight into human nature still resonates. It is no less true in the twenty-first century United States than in the first-century Roman Empire that most of the evils and distractions of the world originate in human hearts warped by anxiety and sin. We are prone to fragmentation by worldly distractions and demands because a prior division exists within ourselves.[2]

Today's anxious persons might find a patron saint in Jesus' friend Martha, whom he chided for being "worried and distracted by many things" (Luke 10:41, NRSV). Like Martha, we are worried about many things: How will I meet my deadline at work this week *and* get the kids to all their extracurriculars? Will I be able to find a job after graduation? Why do all my Facebook friends seem to be having more fun than I am? We operate under the illusion that accomplishing all these things will make us happy when more often than not they distract us from what would actually fulfill us. Jesus' advice to Martha (and to us) is that "there is need of only one thing" (Luke 10:42, NRSV). To heal our fragmented inner lives, we must set our hearts on that one necessary thing.

In his exchange with a lawyer earlier in the same chapter, Jesus specified what this one thing is: "You shall love the Lord your God with all your heart, and with all your soul, and with all your strength, and with all your mind" (Luke 10:27; cf. 10:41, NRSV). God alone can satisfy the longings of the human heart because God created us for love, which is to say that God created us for Himself, who is love (1 John 4:8). To receive fully God's gift of love requires that we give of ourselves in love, but this is a difficult thing. For that reason we pursue many lesser substitutes for love like honor,

1. See Matt 6:34; Luke 12:22; John 14:27.
2. Cf. Rom 7:15; Paul VI, "Gaudium et Spes," no. 10.

popularity, and power. But because none of these substitutes is sufficient in itself, we are always seeking something more. The result is that we end up being pulled in many different directions. When we turn from unity in God, we fall into a "state of disintegration."[3]

In contrast, the person who has clarity about what matters most—the "pure of heart" as Jesus calls them—are those who set their hearts fully on God. This purity of heart is the key to internal peace and contentment, as Jesus suggests when he includes it among his Beatitudes: "Blessed are the pure of heart, for they shall see God" (Matt 5:8).

"SEEING" AS MEANING-MAKING AND SEEING AS JESUS SEES

This beatitude illuminates the inseparable connection between desiring and seeing, a connection confirmed by research in psychology and cognitive science. Like other animals, we human beings perceive our external environment when sensory receptors on the surface of the body receive impressions from outside, which they relay through sensory and motor nerves to the brain.[4] The firing of the brain's neurons in different patterns corresponding to external stimuli provide the physiological basis for mental "images."[5] So long as we are awake or dreaming, we experience a constant stream of images through our consciousness, which constitutes the main content of our thoughts. The ability to generate and attend to these images is what we describe as our "imagination" in the most basic sense of the word.[6]

However, we also "see" reality in another sense that goes beyond an animal's capacity for sight. As the oft-cited Talmudic dictum goes, "We do not see things as they are; we see them as we are." We are not content to perceive shapes and light; we seek meaning in what we perceive. We desire to understand why things are the way they are. In this sense, our efforts to

---

3. Augustine, *Confessions*, II.i(1).

4. Johnson, *Body in the Mind*; cf. Aquinas, *De Veritate*, q.2, a.3, arg. 19.[1].

5. My use of "image" is consistent with that of neuroscientist Antonio Damasio, which diverges from popular usage. For Damasio, the word "images" indicates "mental patterns with a structure built with the tokens of each of the sensory modalities—visual, auditory, olfactory, gustatory, and somatosensory" (*Feeling of What Happens*, 318). Significant in Damasio's definition is the fact that the term "image" is not limited to the visual.

6. This basic definition of imagination is in line with that employed by Mary Warnock in *Imagination*.

make meaning of reality are shot through with affectivity from the start.[7] What we see elicits certain feelings and desires, and what we desire influences what and how we see.

We are able to "see" more than the eye perceives thanks to what psychologists call the "symbolic function," the mental capacity for associating mental images with things other than the physical objects to which they correspond.[8] A red, octagonal sign on the street corner is not just a visual curiosity to us. We know that it means we should stop. Besides creating words that carry a direct correspondence between sign and referent, we also create "symbols" that eschew a single, clearly defined meaning. Because of their capacity to bear meaning that is imprecisely understood, symbols play a crucial role in the human search for meaning. They make possible the integration of diverse ideas, impressions, feelings, and experiences that defy conceptual synthesis. In the words of Avery Dulles (drawing on the work of Michael Polanyi), symbols "arouse tacit awareness of things too vast, subtle, or complex to be grasped in an explicit way."[9]

Tacit, symbolic thinking proves essential for negotiating the concrete demands of living in a world that always exceeds our intellectual grasp. With comprehensive understanding of reality beyond our reach, we have to utilize the symbols at hand in order to orient ourselves in the world and to relate to that which we understand only vaguely. Typically, we borrow these symbols from the common fund of the community in which we grow up. Three "master images" or "master symbols" in particular—our self-image, God-image, and world-image—enable us to envision a life for ourselves.[10] We make connections between these core symbols and other meaningful symbols drawn from our communities, traditions, and personal experiences (e.g., friend, enemy, success, home), thereby imaginatively forging the diverse aspects of our lived experience into a cohesive whole. The resulting symbol system enables us to achieve a sense of coherence and personal integration even as we lack perfect knowledge of the world. This imaginative capacity is what enables us, in the words of Craig Dykstra, to "attend to the deep meaning of things," to experience life as meaningful and whole.[11]

---

7. See Kegan, *Evolving Self,* 83; Haidt, *Righteous Mind.*

8. Piaget and Inhelder, *Psychology of the Child,* 51

9. Dulles, *Models of Revelation,* 257.

10. Schneiders, *Revelatory Text,* 104. This dimension of the imagination is what Richard Côte forefronts in his book on faith and imagination, *Lazarus! Come Out!*

11. Dykstra, "Pastoral and Ecclesial Imagination," 48.

We shape these core symbols and a holistic vision of reality in accord with our personal experiences and concerns and those of the communities that nurture us. If we approach the world with a closed heart, we see little love in the world. If we are divided within ourselves, the world appears a chaotic place. By contrast, if we approach reality with purity of heart, as Jesus does, we are able to see reality differently. If we set our hearts on God, who is love, and make love the central concern of our lives, we come to see reality through the eyes of love. This transformed way of seeing reality inevitably transforms a person's master symbols of God, self, and world.

Most people have some God-image, whether that image is of a mysterious Force that infuses the universe, a powerful being residing in heaven, or an image of absence, the negation of some God-image. When looking at reality through the lens of Jesus' teaching, we come to know God as a Father who loves us (John 16:27). God knows us even more intimately than our own parents and wants to be known intimately by us as "Abba" (Daddy) (Rom 8:15, NRSV). Like a loving parent who wants only good things for their child, God knows our needs and is responsive to our requests (Matt 6:8, 26; 7:11; Luke 11:13; John 16:23). Like a merciful father who has been insulted and disgraced by an ungrateful son, God is always willing to welcome us back into God's presence and even to condescend to meet us when we are still a long way off (Luke 6:36; 15:11–32). God's care and loving kindness extend in a special way to the vulnerable, to the "little ones" whom society despises, mistreats, and ignores (Matt 18:10–14, NRSV). Finally, through Jesus, we come to know God as the God of life, the one who gives life and who restores life to the dead (John 5:21). God does this, Jesus explains, because God loves us and wants us to share in God's own life (Luke 12:32; John 14:2).

To know God as the Son knows the Father is also to see ourselves in a different light, that is, to form a different self-image. First and foremost, knowing God as the loving Father means knowing ourselves as God's beloved children (Matt 5:9, 45). Because all human beings are God's children, we are truly brothers and sisters to one another (Matt 12:50; Luke 8:21). Jesus invites us to love our neighbor as ourselves (Matt 22:39; Mark 12:31), thus closely linking our self-image with our image of the "other." In the light of God's love, our faults become more apparent to us. Yet, though aware of our sinfulness, we also know ourselves as loved sinners. We see ourselves in the prodigal son, who sins against his father and yet, when he turns back on his sin, is shown mercy and even granted a new dignity (Luke 15:11–32). Although truly indebted to God for all that we have and are, God does not regard us as slaves, as did the Greek gods. Instead God has called us friends (John 15:15).

Our world-image encapsulates how we envision the world as a whole. Because each of us has a unique set of experiences, knowledge, and concerns, we live in a different "world" from others, even our neighbors and classmates who occupy the same physical environment. One person who grew up in a loving household might envision the world as the common home of the human family. Another person who works seventy hours a week in a competitive workplace might see the world as a jungle in which everyone has to look out for himself and only the fit survive. Seeing reality through Jesus' eyes likewise shapes our world-image. Precisely how, we will examine in the next section.

If symbols like our God-image, self-image, and world-image provide the bare bones of meaning, stories are what put muscle and flesh on those bones and set them in motion. The stories that we are told and that we tell ourselves build upon our master symbols, fleshing out our understanding of ourselves, the world in which we live, and our relation to the transcendent.[12] We see ourselves as part of a national story of working hard to realize the American dream or a cosmic story of an ongoing battle between forces of good and evil. These stories are not always explicit. We absorb them from overhearing snippets of our parents' conversations about religion and politics, from the TV shows and advertisements we watch, and from the rituals of daily life.

Our foundational stories set up a "worldview" for us.[13] A person's worldview encompasses not only their world-image but also, more comprehensively, their holistic perception of and affective disposition toward reality as they experience it.[14] For most of us, our worldview operates on a pre-theoretical, imaginative level, which is to say that it is constituted by the unspoken assumptions and feelings about reality that underlie our

12. Paul Ricoeur and others have so compellingly established the importance of narrative for human beings that I need not belabor the point. See Ricoeur, *Time and Narrative*; McAdams, *Redemptive Self*; Holstein and Gubrium, *Self We Live By*.

13. Cf. Tilley, *Faith*, 76.

14. The term *Weltanschauung* (typically translated as "worldview" in English) has a long, complex history, which receives thorough treatment in David Naugle's *Worldview*. As Naugle explains, the concept has been variously defined, some scholars describing it as an intellectual construct while others include sensory and affective dimensions. My usage is consistent with that of van der Kooij et al., "'Worldview.'"

stated beliefs rather than the reasons we might give to justify those beliefs. Because we live in a "world" that is partially a mental construction, our worldviews determine how each of us experiences the events of our lives and what we understand our life to be about.

JESUS' WORLDVIEW AND THE REIGN OF GOD

How and what Jesus taught out of his own vision of the world has decisively shaped the way Christians throughout history have seen the world. Although there is much to be said about the various understandings of the "world" that emerge from the New Testament and the world-images implicit therein, we will focus our attention on what is most central to Jesus' worldview, namely, seeing the world as the ground of the inbreaking of the reign of God.[15]

Although the reign of God constitutes the central focus of Jesus' preaching, he never offered a precise definition or description of it. His usage of *basileia tou theou* primarily denotes God's activity in shaping human experience. While this term can be translated as the "kingdom," "reign," or "rule" of God, Jesus' emphasis on God's activity makes "reign" or "rule" more appropriate translations than the more static "kingdom." According to Jesus, God's reigning or activity in the world involves, among other things, casting out evil elements (Matt 12:28; Luke 11:20), liberating the captive, healing the infirm (Matt 11:5; Luke 7:22), and raising the dead (Matt 11:5).

Rather than offering descriptive statements of God's reign, Jesus preferred to speak of it analogically through parables. What vision emerges in these parables? To begin with, the parables reveal that the world is not as it should be. The world is like a field into which an enemy has crept and sown weeds among the crops (Matt 13:24–30). As a result, we experience the world as a mix of good and evil. Because the world has been corrupted by sin, the inbreaking of God's reign will involve reversal of the accustomed order of things, like a landowner who gives the same payment to workers arriving late as to those who began early (Matt 20:1–13). Jesus' parables also suggest that God's reign pervades this world and yet remains imperceptible, at least to some. Like a bit of yeast hidden in a huge batch of flour, it easily escapes notice while nonetheless having a profoundly transformative effect (Matt 13:33). Such images lead one who looks at the world as Jesus does to

15. For a discussion of these various meanings, see Schneiders, *Buying the Field*, chapter 1.

expect to encounter mystery and wonder in the ordinariness of the world. In this "sacramental" worldview, the things of this world take on the significance of signs pointing to a higher reality.

Jesus' parables also reveal the giftedness of the world. The world and our very existence are not the result of our own efforts. Like a seed that grows into a plant overnight, this world and the reign of God are given to us and we know not how (Mark 4:26–27). To live in the world in which God reigns is to receive life gratefully as a gratuitous gift rather than apprehensively attempting to seize control of it for ourselves, as Adam and Eve did and as fallen human beings tend to do. It is to recognize God's sovereignty and to participate in the universal peace, justice, and love that God wills (Matt 6:9–13; Luke 11:2–4).

Jesus invites his audience to recognize God's activity within their own lives: "Nor will they say, 'Look, here it is!' or 'There it is!' For, in fact, the kingdom of God is among [or within] you" (Luke 17:20–21, NRSV). In this sense, even though God's reign is not coterminous with the world, we can encounter it in the world. We can experience it individually within ourselves but especially in community. In response to a question about God's reign, Jesus assures his disciples, "Where two or three are gathered in my name, I am there among them" (Matt 18:20, NRSV).

To enter Jesus' vision of reality in which God reigns supremely and lovingly is to enter into the community that shares and is constituted by that vision. It is to recognize that we never make meaning alone but rather are always participating in a communal enterprise. The term "imaginary"—used prominently by philosopher Charles Taylor—captures this communal dynamic of meaning-making.[16] Like an individual's worldview, an imaginary is not to be confused with a body of theories about the universe; rather, it is the sum total of a community's collective, pre-theoretical assumptions about the nature of the cosmos (the "cosmic imaginary") and society (the "social imaginary"). It is what the community simply takes for granted about the way things are. The communal imaginary is both a source of cohesion and a basic fund of meaning for the community and all its members. For Christians, participating in the Christian community's common vision of reality inspired by Jesus is essential to the life of discipleship.

16. Taylor, *Secular Age*, 146.

JESUS' INVITATION TO CONVERSION

We human beings never see reality simply "as it is." For one thing, we make meaning out of the world we encounter in concert with the communities that nurture us. For another, our desiring influences our seeing. If we are pure of heart—that is, if the primary object of our desire is the one truly necessary thing, namely, God—we will see the world through the eyes of love. Unfortunately, we struggle to achieve this purity of heart in a fallen world. Affected as we all are by sin, we struggle to see the world in this way. Too often, we approach the world with a closed heart and so see little love in the world. Too often, we are divided within ourselves and so see the world as a chaotic, conflictual place.

Jesus saw clearly that the problems of the world spring from distorted human hearts and imaginations. Accordingly, his prescription for healing the world did not focus on new ordinances or social structures. Rather, he called first and foremost for interior transformation or "conversion"—a transformation of what we love, how we look at reality, and, subsequently, our way of being in the world. Only by setting our whole heart on God and allowing that pure desire to shape our worldview can we as divided persons become whole and live life to the full (John 10:10). Jesus summed up this invitation to total transformation in the central proclamation of his ministry: "The kingdom of God has come near; repent [or be converted], and believe in the good news" (Mark 1:15; Matt 4:17, NRSV).

This is not an easy invitation to accept. Jesus is inviting us to change fundamentally our most deeply ingrained concerns and assumptions about reality. Because the human psyche tends to resist anything so profoundly destabilizing, we typically undergo change of this magnitude only when we have a powerful experience or are confronted with something that we cannot explain within our present framework. Arguments and discursive reasoning, by contrast, are generally ineffective at prompting such radical change because the human mind is quite ingenious at twisting evidence and arguments to justify an accustomed way of seeing things. If real change is to occur, the very foundation of our meaning, of our worldview, must be transformed. That is to say we must, in the words of Jesus, "be converted."

We will discuss the phenomenon of conversion in more depth in chapter 3. For now, the important thing to examine is how Jesus prompted the radical change of heart and mind needed for people to recognize the reign of God breaking into the world. He made use of a variety of methods, including proverbs, parenetical sayings, beatitudes, apocalyptic images, and prophetic words and gestures. Generally speaking, however, it seems Jesus preferred showing to telling. His first move is typically not to lecture but rather to invite his audience to "come and see" (John 1:39, NRSV), usually by telling them a story, a parable.

A parable is "a metaphor or simile drawn from nature or common life, arresting the hearer by its vividness or strangeness, leaving the mind in sufficient doubt about its precise application to tease it into active thought."[17] As opposed to more didactic forms of teaching, parables engage us on multiple levels. Scripture scholar Pheme Perkins explains, "We respond to a parable on many levels with our minds, with our feelings, and perhaps even with an unconscious resonance to its archetypal themes. Such levels of response," she adds, "are the ground of any conversion."[18] Prompting a total transformation requires engaging people in the fullness of their being. By examining the dynamics of Jesus' parables, we can better understand how they facilitate a total conversion to the reign of God.

WHAT PARABLES DO TO US AND HOW THEY DO IT

We can consistently discern three movements in Jesus' parables: First, he stimulates the audience's imaginations. Next, he disrupts and expands their accustomed way of seeing things. Finally, he invites them to embrace a new way of seeing. Let's look at how this dynamic plays out in one of Jesus' most famous parables, the parable of the good Samaritan.

First, Jesus engages his audience's imaginations with the familiar. The events he describes in his parables correspond to the everyday activities of his hearers—casting nets in the sea, laboring in the vineyard, baking bread, shepherding sheep, or, in the case of the parable of the good Samaritan, walking the road between their hometowns and Jerusalem to worship in the temple. His audience would have known the way well. The first words of the story in Luke 10:29 ("A man was going down from Jerusalem to Jericho . . . " [NRSV]) would have activated his audience's imaginations. In the way that someone mentioning the daily commute to work or school immediately brings to our minds images of familiar landmarks along our usual route, each person listening to Jesus would have pictured this road that they had walked many times. The feelings of familiarity intensify as Jesus continues: " . . . and fell into the hands of robbers" (v. 29, NRSV).

17. Dodd, *Parables of the Kingdom*, 10.
18. Perkins, *Hearing the Parables of Jesus*, 4.

The road between Jericho and Jerusalem was known to be a dangerous one. Jesus' words might have brought to mind specific bends in the road or outcroppings of rocks that his audience members approached cautiously when making their way along this road, fearing that robbers might be lying in wait. The mention of a priest coming along would likewise be expected. Jesus' audience frequently would have encountered priests heading up to the temple or returning home after completing their service.

We like what is familiar, and we care more about stories that concern ourselves. By beginning with familiar concerns and images, within the space of a few brief sentences, Jesus has drawn his audience in.

Then comes the unexpected. As Jesus expands the story's familiar cast of characters one at a time, his audience's imaginations would have raced ahead. First comes the priest and then a Levite. His Jewish audience would have anticipated the next character, an Israelite, the third member of the trio so commonplace in the Hebrew Scriptures. It would have thus come as a surprise when a Samaritan appears instead. Scripture scholar Amy-Jill Levine playfully suggests, "In modern terms, this would be like going from Larry and Moe to Osama bin Laden."[19] Levine's quip hints at another reason Jesus' introduction of the Samaritan would have surprised his audience. It is not the priest or the Levite who helps the injured man but a Samaritan, a member of a group reviled by the Jews after centuries of religious conflict. If Jesus were telling this parable in the modern-day United States, he might substitute a prominent figure in the opposing political party, whose very name would make our blood boil. By making the Samaritan the hero of the story, Jesus invites his audience to stretch their hearts and imaginations to include this hated group within the category of "neighbor."

This kind of imaginative disruption is a hallmark of Jesus' parables. He told parables with the intention of questioning his audience's desires and shaking them out of their accustomed ways of seeing things. Walter Conn describes the parables' effect eloquently: "Having robbed us of the certainties of our given world, they would leave us at the brink of relativity, naked and totally vulnerable before the divine mystery that is God."[20]

At the end of the parable of the good Samaritan (and most parables), Jesus confronts his audience with a decision. He asks his audience (primarily the lawyer), "Which of these three, do you think, was a neighbor to the man who fell into the hands of the robbers?" and then challenges him, "Go

19. Levine, *Short Stories by Jesus*, 95.
20. Conn, *Christian Conversion*, 214.

and do likewise" (Luke 10:36–37, NRSV). Will the lawyer identify with the priest and Levite, people who are like himself but who passed by a man in need, or with the Samaritan, a member of a despised outgroup who acted with compassion? This choice is fraught with emotion. Jesus' audience is torn between allegiance to tribe and basic compassion for a fellow human being in need. The choice is also a choice between an accustomed way of seeing things and a new way. Neither is an easy choice. The former way of imagining was too easy, too narrow, but the alternative makes no sense within the worldview of a first-century Jew whose image of neighbor includes only fellow Jews and who sees Samaritans as enemies. In the same way, many of us today struggle to see someone with political or religious leanings opposed to our own as anything other than a symbol of all that is wrong with the world. Our minds reel as we try to make sense of the alternative view Jesus proposes to us.

In this manner, Jesus' parables lead his audience imaginatively from the familiar, through the shocking, to a choice about how to make sense of the reality presented to them. Parables do not merely illustrate things about reality that could be explained in more straightforward terms. In fact, Jesus' parables often seem to have the opposite effect, leaving people disoriented and confused.[21] This is not a pedagogical shortcoming but rather the intended effect of the parable. When the topic is the reign of God, all concepts and reasonings prove inadequate because, as Bruce Chilton explains, "the kingdom of God is not merely a concept, but a task that is ever more necessary."[22] If the reign of God is not a place or a concept but rather God's own activity, then we can know God's reign only by participating in it. Jesus' parables do not merely describe the reign of God; they draw us into an experience of it. They elicit our active imagining and a lived response in a way that concepts and arguments cannot.

This is what Levine means when she writes that in order to understand the meaning of Jesus' parables, one must "take them seriously not as 'meaning' but as soliciting our meaning making."[23] The deepest meaning of the parable lies not in what it says but rather in what it does to us. Parables are better understood as exercises of the heart and imagination than as ethical lessons. They shake us out of distorted desiring and closed thinking and invite us to join Jesus in actively envisioning a new reality that God is

---

21. See, for example, Mark 4:10–13; Matt 13:10–11; 15:15–16; Luke 8:9.

22. Chilton, "Kingdom of God," 522.

23. Levine, Short Stories by Jesus, 276.

bringing into being before our very eyes. They train us, first, to regularly smash our idolatrous images of God and remain open to God's ongoing self-revelation. They train us to see not only ourselves but all others as God sees us, namely, as beloved children. Finally, they train us to keep seeing the world anew, remaining open to God's activity breaking into our lives in ever new and unexpected ways.

In sum, Jesus' parables train us to receive attentively as well as construct actively our meaning, to make our meaning-making a collaborative participation in God's ongoing revelation of reality rather than settling for the narrow meaning that we can give to our own lives.[24] Making our way through life with an open-ended worldview is uncomfortable. We much prefer to have things settled. However, Jesus' parables offer a model of how we can be shaken out of our complacent ways of seeing things and open ourselves to a conversion in our imagining. The promise implicit in Jesus' parables is if we can abide a period of wandering through the wilderness of the imagination, we will one day find ourselves drinking from an inexhaustible wellspring of meaning.

IMITATING JESUS' EXAMPLE AMIDST CULTURAL CHANGE

Jesus' teachings have continued to gain a hearing down through the centuries because he spoke to the fundamental concerns of human existence—our yearnings for peace, meaning, and fulfillment. Speaking to these concerns, he taught that the real obstacles to fulfillment stem from problems of the heart and imagination. Accordingly, when he entered the world to save humanity, he did not come to vanquish enemy armies or overthrow rival kings. Instead, he invited humanity into the path to healing that passes through interior transformation (that is, conversion).

We have just seen how Jesus extended this invitation to conversion in large part through telling parables of the reign of God. While inviting our active imagining, Jesus' vision of the reign of God also gives definitive direction to our efforts to make sense of reality. It molds the master symbols

---

24. By now it should be clear that I understand human meaning-making as a collaborative endeavor rather than the autonomous activity of individuals. Although I will continue to use the language of "meaning-making" and "meaning-maker" throughout this book, I do so reluctantly for the sake of readability and with the caveat that these phrases for me carry the connotation of a collaborative activity.

that orient us in the world and serve as focal reference points for our mean-ing-making. We inevitably refine the meanings carried by these symbols with the aid of concepts and arguments, but it is only insofar as personal beliefs and the church's doctrines continue to draw upon the power of these symbols that our individual and communal imagining remains faithful to Jesus' vision of the reign of God.[25]

Notwithstanding the permanent validity of Jesus' vision, the Chris-tian imagination can and must evolve. The world has changed signifi-cantly since Jesus' time, and every generation faces new challenges that Jesus did not explicitly address. Furthermore, even though Jesus made in-ner transformation possible in an unprecedented and unrepeatable way, it remains a task for each individual to undergo a personal conversion. This task of issuing the timeless call to conversion in a way that meets the particular challenges of the present historical moment constitutes the mission of the church in the world.

In the following chapter we will examine the particular challenges of our own era. However, before doing so, it might instill some confidence to note that we are not the first to have to seek new ways of remaining united with Christ in the face of changing cultural circumstances. This is something Christians have had to struggle with since the beginning, and often it was a renewed focus on the interior life that helped the church to stay faithful to its mission in different times and cultures.

In the years immediately following Jesus' ascension, the first Christians had to figure out what to do now that Jesus was gone. Eventually they came to make sense of their new reality, in the first place, through their experience of encountering Christ in the Eucharist. The story of the two disciples on the road to Emmaus (Luke 24:13–35) dramatizes this breakthrough in the nascent Christian community. The writings of Saint Paul and later of Saint Augustine provide evidence of how early Christians encountered the risen Christ's presence within themselves.[26] In the third and fourth centuries, the desert fathers and mothers would develop practices of contemplative prayer aimed at cultivating awareness of Christ's presence within.

The turn of the sixteenth century was another period of dramatic change for Christians and all of the Western world. At that time, explor-ers like Bartolomeu Dias, Christopher Columbus, and Ferdinand Magellan were extending the horizons of the known world. Reformers like Martin

---

25. Cf. Dulles, *Models of Revelation*, 161.

26. See Gal 2:20; Augustine, *Confessions*, IV.xii(19), respectively.

Luther, Huldrych Zwingli, and John Calvin were upending the Christian world by challenging the established traditions and doctrines of the Catholic Church. Once again, in the face of rapidly changing circumstances, great saints helped Christians remain stable in Christ by turning to their own inner depths. Saint Ignatius of Loyola, for example, developed detailed processes for the "discernment of spirits," interpreting where God or the evil spirit may be at work in the interior movements of one's thoughts, imaginings, feelings, and desires.[27] More people may be familiar with the Ignatian "examen," a daily examination of conscience (or consciousness—both are appropriate translations of Ignatius's language) in which the individual mentally replays the day, repenting of missed opportunities to love and giving thanks for blessings received.

The work of spiritual renewal continued after Ignatius's death in persons like Teresa of Avila and John of the Cross. Teresa's *Interior Castle* maps out the interior life in intimate detail, leading the reader on the journey of the soul's growth toward God through earlier stages of ascetic practices and active prayer and later stages of passive, contemplative prayer. John of the Cross likewise delved into the intricacies of the interior life in writings such as *The Dark Night of the Soul* and *Ascent of Mount Carmel*. Coming at a time when there was much to distract Christians from their relationship with Christ, the writings of these two saints represented a new level of attentiveness to mystical experience and the interior life.

I might cite many more examples from Christian history like those above. However, my point is not to provide an exhaustive history but rather to establish the precedent for the kind of interior renewal that has become necessary in our own day. Looking to the early church and to Reformation-era contemplatives, we find models for how the church carries on its mission of inviting conversion in the face of new cultural challenges.

CONCLUSION

At their core, the most serious challenges Christians face today are the same as those Jesus' first followers confronted. We experience our lives as fragmented because we desire many things instead of the one thing that truly satisfies. We suffer confusion and misunderstandings because we look at the world through eyes of self-interest rather than eyes of love. The

---

27. Ignatius of Loyola, *Spiritual Exercises*.

solution in its most basic form is to undergo an inner conversion of our desiring and imagining.

Jesus provides religious educators with a model of how to invite this conversion. However, as we have just seen, remaining faithful to Jesus' mission often requires creative adaptation to changing cultural circumstances. This has been the case at key moments in the church's history, and it is certainly the case in our present day and culture, which is markedly different from the context in which Jesus taught. In the next chapter, we will explore the unique challenges of the present historical moment and discuss the new form of interiority that Christians will need to continue drawing life from Jesus' vision of the reign of God in today's world.

chapter 2

POST-MODERN CHALLENGES
TO FULLNESS OF LIFE

Christians today are confronted with the same fundamental challenge that Christians have faced since Jesus' time. Distorted desires of the heart and imaginings of the mind lead us astray from the life of fullness and intimacy with God that God intends for us. As Joseph Ratzinger once wrote, "If today we are scarcely able any longer to become aware of God, that is because we find it so easy to evade ourselves. . . . Our own interior depths remain closed to us. If it is true that a man can see only with his heart, then how blind we all are!"[1] The solution Jesus offers us is to undergo a conversion that will reorient and re-integrate our lives. True to that promise, countless people throughout history have experienced healing and wholeness by heeding Jesus' call to conversion and interior renewal.

We saw at the end of the previous chapter that every age brings changes to which the church must adapt if it is to fulfill its mission of inviting people to the inner transformation that leads to communion with God. The present age is no exception. What is new about the present era is that, to a degree unprecedented in the history of Christianity, many people are failing to find meaning in or see the relevance of Christianity for their lives. Some have responded by leaving the church of their youth. Others remain, although given current trends, we might wonder for how long and with what level of investment. For both of these groups and for many others along the spectrum of unbelief, a void of meaning has opened up in their lives. How did this happen? How did the Christian

1. Ratzinger, *Faith and the Future*, 114–15.

imaginary, which for centuries was virtually all-encompassing in the Western world, become so eviscerated?

In the introduction, I adverted to the work of Charles Taylor, who addresses this question with a wide-ranging account of sweeping cultural transformations transpiring over the course of several centuries. Rich in detail and highly compelling in its argumentation, Taylor's text has become an essential reference point in current discussions of religion and secularization. Still, although *A Secular Age* is most illuminating, the process of secularization Taylor describes is so subtle and pervasive that religious educators might despair of identifying a concrete place to begin mounting a response. With centuries of sundry cultural forces eroding the shores of faith, what hope do religious communities have of counteracting the dissipation of meaning experienced by fellow believers like my student David, whose struggles I recounted in the introduction?

Without denying the daunting nature of the problem, I believe it possible to couch the problem in more comprehensible terms. My intention in the present chapter is to zoom in on the experience of the individual who is living the fragilized, "cross-pressured" existence Taylor describes to examine how people in a secular age make meaning or fail to do so.[2] In other words, I want to examine how these historic changes impact the lives of individual persons as well as society as a whole. In so doing I hope to arrive at a more personal understanding of the obstacles that stand between contemporary persons and the life in abundance that Jesus promises. At the end of the chapter, we will have occasion to discuss why Jesus' call to interior conversion remains a necessary part of the solution as well as why Christian interiority will need to take a different form than it did for people of ages past.

PSYCHOLOGICAL PERSPECTIVES ON THE MEANINGFULNESS OF LIFE

In my efforts to understand what has changed since Jesus' time and how it has affected the lives of contemporary Christians, I have been greatly aided by research in the field of developmental psychology. Referring back to the previous chapter will help me to explain why.

When examining Jesus' teaching, I touched upon some important aspects of the process by which humans make meaning. We saw that meaning

2. Taylor, *Secular Age*, 304.

is not a given, that we actively construct the meaning that gives coherence and direction to our lives. Because meaning is not a given, we can fail to make meaning or lose a sense of life's meaningfulness. Psychological research tells us that, if our meaning framework or worldview is weakened, our mental health becomes more susceptible to deterioration when we confront significant change or disorienting experiences (as we almost inevitably do in today's world).[3] Conversely, we experience a sense of well-being on account of feeling that life is relatively predictable and our ability to synthesize mentally a more or less stable worldview (what psychologist Aaron Antonovsky calls "sense of coherence").[4] Naturally, the human psyche wants to maintain this state of integration and equilibrium.

Despite the human psyche's powerful drive for stability, the work of making meaning is so complex and demanding that breakdowns are virtually inevitable. Adaptation is thus an essential function of human psychology.[5] Most of the time, these breakdowns are minor and temporary. For example, a child's understanding of the world may be temporarily thrown into disarray when she encounters people who speak a different language or observes customs different from those of her family. Such new information she can process within her existing mental framework after a relatively brief period of confusion. Jean Piaget, the founding father of developmental psychology, described this kind of mental adaptation as "assimilation."[6] Sometimes the disruption is more significant. People occasionally encounter things they cannot understand within their existing worldview. In such cases their mental framework itself must change in order to make sense of or "accommodate" this new experience and maintain psychological equilibrium.[7]

It was the central insight of Piaget that we as human beings predictably undergo radical changes in the structure of our thinking several times throughout our lives. According to Piaget, every change in the structure of our thinking ushers in a new "period" or "stage" of cognitive development, each of which represents a qualitatively different way of constructing meaning. It is a change not merely in *what* we think but rather in *how* we

---

3. See Frankl, *Man's Search for Meaning*; Antonovsky, *Unraveling the Mystery of Health*; cf. Berger, *Sacred Canopy*, 22.

4. Antonovsky, *Unraveling the Mystery of Health*.

5. Piaget and Inhelder, *Psychology of the Child*.

6. Piaget and Inhelder, *Psychology of the Child*, 6.

7. Piaget and Inhelder, *Psychology of the Child*, 6.

think. Since Piaget's landmark discovery, researchers have theorized distinct stages in various realms of human development, including the development of the ego,[8] the self,[9] moral reasoning,[10] and faith.[11] Although more recent research has cast doubt upon the theory of sequential developmental stages, virtually no psychologist today would deny that the maturation of the brain and additional life experience reliably give rise to mental capacities that a person did not and could not possess earlier in life.

Understanding this dynamic of human psychology sheds some light on the crises of faith and meaning that many people are experiencing today. When our development does not keep pace with the mental challenges we encounter in daily life, we struggle to make sense of the world and, as a result, experience psychological disequilibrium that manifests in anxiety and other mental health issues. Robert Kegan, a successor of Piaget in the field of developmental psychology, explains these dynamics in terms of the "differentiation" and "re-integration" of consciousness.[12] At certain times in our development we emerge from *embeddedness in* particular meanings to an *awareness of* those meanings. This is what Kegan means by "differentiation." Until and unless we achieve a new integration that reconciles old and new meanings within a new mental framework (what Kegan calls "evolutionary balances"[13] or "orders of consciousness"[14]), we will experience varying degrees of psychological dis-ease.

Inadequate development becomes a more widespread problem in times of significant cultural change. The research Kegan presents in *In Over Our Heads* suggests we are currently living in such a time. The demands of twenty first-century living are exceeding the capacity of many of us to make sense of it all. In this book I extend Kegan's analysis by arguing that this mismatch between the mental demands of current culture and people's meaning-making capacities is a major reason why many people like my student David are struggling to find meaning in their faith tradition or in life in general. As we saw in the previous chapter, this is not the first time cultural developments have made it necessary for Christians to undergo a development in the way

8. Erikson, *Childhood and Society.*

9. Kegan, *Evolving Self.*

10. Kohlberg, *Psychology of Moral Development*; Gilligan, *In a Different Voice.*

11. Fowler, *Stages of Faith.*

12. Kegan, *Evolving Self.*

13. Kegan, *Evolving Self*, 85.

14. Kegan, *In Over Our Heads*, 10.

they make sense of faith. However, the current development is in certain respects unlike anything that has come before.

One particular thread in developmental research brings into relief what is different about recent cultural changes. Across various theorists' development frameworks, one can consistently discern the basic contours of at least three general forms of meaning-making corresponding roughly to what Paul Ricoeur terms "pre-critical," "critical," and "post-critical" thinking.[15] Scholars like Robert Kegan and Bernard Lonergan have discerned these forms of meaning-making not only in the development of individuals but also in the development of cultures.[16] Analyzing different historical eras within this developmental framework enables us to identify significant changes in societies over time and how those changes affect the people living within those societies.

In the following sections I will examine each of the pre-critical, critical, and post-critical forms of meaning-making as they might manifest in the life of a person who has experienced the deterioration of her religious worldview. In order to give this psychological framework concreteness, I will describe this developmental process as experienced by a fictional young woman named Serena. Serena's story embodies different aspects of the stories of former students and other people I have encountered who are presently failing to find meaning in the faith of their ancestors. By following the course of Serena's development, we will be able to observe how existential and cultural challenges prompt evolution to new ways of making meaning and in this way attempt to shed some light on our current crisis of faith and meaning.

PRE-CRITICAL MEANING-MAKING

Manifestation in the Individual[17]

The defining trait of a pre-critical meaning-maker (i.e., a person operating out of pre-critical consciousness) is a lack of awareness of their own meaning-making. Such a person takes at face value the meaning that presents

---

15. Ricoeur, *Symbolism of Evil*, 352.

16. Cf. Kegan, *In Over Our Heads*, 11.

17. The account of pre-critical meaning-making that I present here parallels Kohlberg's and Gilligan's pre-conventional and conventional stages of moral reasoning, Fowler's stages of faith zero to three, and Kegan's orders of consciousness one to four.

itself to consciousness. What seems to be is simply what is. Such an uncomplicated worldview enables this person to enjoy a relatively undisturbed sense of life's fullness as well as the psychological integration afforded by undifferentiated consciousness.

At the start of her life Serena sees the world through naïve eyes. Her initial experience of the world is that of raw sight, sound, smell, and touch. However, her imaginative capacities soon begin to develop, enabling her to employ signs and bring to mind objects that are not immediately present. During her early childhood, the fantastical imaginings in her head seem every bit as real as the real-world objects she can see and touch. With images of monsters from storybooks swimming in her head, she is convinced that some of them are lurking under her bed.

In time and with the benefit of additional social interaction and cognitive development, Serena eventually assumes some degree of control over her imagination. Her parents assure her that there is no monster under the bed, older kids make fun of her for believing in Santa Claus, and so these images are relegated to the closet of childhood. In this way Serena's vision of reality increasingly reflects not just what she sees but also what "we" see. This movement into a more "conventional" mode of thinking thus constitutes a sort of transition or halfway point between pre-critical and critical meaning-making.[18]

Despite the imposition of new communal checks on her fantastical imagining, Serena's meaning-making remains largely uncritical at this point in her development insofar as her thinking still lacks critical questioning and reasoning about the phenomena presented to her consciousness. In the words of Sharon Daloz Parks, pre-critical meaning-makers like Serena "cannot stand outside their own perspective, or reflect upon their own thought."[19] This can be true of adults as well as children. Adults' formerly uninhibited perceptions and imaginings tend to be filtered through the norms of their community. However, many adults take for granted the beliefs and imaginary of the community in the same way that they took for granted the objects of their own imagination as children. Since the friends and family of Serena's parents all take God's existence and the unerring truth of the Bible for granted, so, too, do her parents. They have a low tolerance for ambiguity, and regard people who dissent

---

18. Kohlberg, *Psychology of Moral Development.*

19. Daloz Parks, *Big Questions, Worthy Dreams,* 55.

from the community as mistaken or crazy. They never seriously consider that things might be otherwise.

It is important to note here that pre-critical meaning-making need not carry a pejorative connotation. Development to any given form of meaning-making or the lack thereof does not necessarily make someone a better or worse person. Indeed, many ancient and contemporary saints have lived from a pre-critical form of consciousness. As we continue our exploration, it will become clear that development is desirable to the extent that it enables a person to meet the mental challenges of their context in such a way that they can live a meaningful life.

Manifestation in Culture

Since cultures are constituted by individual human beings, we see pre-critical consciousness—and all forms of consciousness, for that matter—expressed collectively in communities and cultures throughout history. For example, in the practices of primordial religion we see the dynamics of this early form of consciousness writ large.[20] When human beings first began to acquire the symbolic function as a species, the world was suddenly charged with meaning and presence. The mountain was no longer just a pile of rocks but the dwelling place of the gods. Humans' sense of "porousness" or vulnerability in the world was heightened as they were now hemmed in on all sides not only by wild beasts and rival tribes but also by gods and evil spirits.[21] Due to the tendency to rely on myth to explain the world rather than systematic, critical inquiry, collective consciousness in this period of cultural evolution often involves a mixture of truth and error. This pre-critical age—the age of "enchantment" Charles Taylor calls it—held sway through early and medieval Christianity and persisted in the Christian West in varying degrees until as recently as five hundred years ago (and persists still in many quarters of the world).[22]

Andrew Delbanco describes how pre-critical consciousness manifested in the United States in its first two hundred years. "In the first phase of our [American] civilization," writes Delbanco, Americans expressed their sense of the purposefulness of life "through a Christian story that gave meaning to suffering and pleasure alike and promised deliverance

20. See Eliade, *Sacred and the Profane.*

21. Taylor, *Secular Age,* 35.

22. Taylor, *Secular Age,* 25.

from death."[23] In this God-centered phase, colonials ascribed nothing to chance; all was within God's providence, from pregnancies to crop yields. Their imagined condition was that of utter dependence on God in a world largely beyond their control.

The Breakdown of Pre-critical Meaning-Making

Pre-critical consciousness breaks down when previously unquestioned beliefs are seriously challenged, as we can see in Serena's case. While never as devout as her parents, Serena was more or less content to attend church with them on Sundays and never thought to question the beliefs of the community. This begins to change for Serena in her first year away at college when she takes a religious studies class with a professor who, rather than reading the Bible through the eyes of faith as her parents and church community do, employs historical-critical methods of interpretation. He contrasts the creation stories of Genesis with scientific accounts of evolution and geological records that make Serena question her theocentric understanding of how the world came to be. Rereading Gospel passages that she had heard a hundred times in church, Serena now notices what seem to be internal contradictions, like conflicting details in the different accounts of Jesus' resurrection.

At the same time that Serena is encountering these intellectual challenges in class, her experiences outside the classroom contribute to the unraveling of her simplistic worldview. Leaving behind her hometown and entering the university community, she is now in daily contact with people representing a diversity of backgrounds, cultures, and beliefs. On a daily basis, conversations in the dormitory and the dining hall bring these differences into relief and challenge her old assumptions. This plurality of perspectives also infiltrates her consciousness by means of her Twitter and Instagram feeds. Minute by minute images of her friends' notions of the good life, inspirational quotes, and other fragments of meaning pour in. These images along with the images she absorbs through the music she listens to and the shows and commercials she streams online continue to populate her imagination until no set of images—not even the religious symbols of her youth—predominates. No discernible center remains.

Serena is experiencing what Kegan describes as a differentiation of consciousness. When her iconoclastic professor and encounters with

23. Delbanco, *Real American Dream*, 4–5.

people of differing beliefs challenge her own, she begins to emerge from embeddedness in assumed meanings to an awareness of the meaning she and others construct. Because her religious upbringing did not provide her with the mental resources to reconcile the contradictions now becoming apparent to her, Serena begins to doubt the naive beliefs and meanings that she has always taken for granted. Overwhelmed with a multitude of meanings, she is unable to identify any particular meaning as superior or truer than the others.

As we will see presently, experiences of disruption like Serena's became commonplace in the age of modernity as the critical thinking of scientists, scholars, and artists came to penetrate the wider culture. New critical modes of inquiry disrupted the homogeneous culture of naiveté that is most hospitable to pre-critical meaning-making. When this homogeneity is disrupted, pre-critical persons either bury their heads in the sand or undergo a personal crisis, which, if embraced, may lead to a new form of meaning-making.

CRITICAL MEANING-MAKING

Manifestation in the Individual[24]

Such an experience of conflicting interpretations of reality or of the fallibility of previously revered authority can be jarring. Serena is initially distraught by her professor's critical approach, but she adapts. In fact, she soon comes to feel that her encounter with historical-critical methods of scholarship has opened her eyes. Likewise, Serena's newfound awareness of the diversity of perspectives among people brings with it an enhanced capacity to enter into perspectives different from her own.

Impressed by the intelligence of her professor, Serena sets about honing her own powers of rational analysis. She begins to exercise more deliberate, reflective judgment, establishing explicit criteria for truth and seeking evidence rather than taking things for granted. She experiences a strong desire to get to the meaning "behind" religious myths and symbols and discards ones that she perceives to be void of any real meaning. The more she thinks about it, the more obvious the internal inconsistencies of the Bible appear to her. It now seems absurd to believe that the Eucharistic

24. The account of critical meaning-making that I present here parallels Fowler's description of stage four, Kegan's fifth order, and (roughly) Kohlberg's stage four.

bread and wine become the body and blood of Christ, which look and taste the same after the consecration as they do before. Serena continues to humor her parents by attending Mass when she returns home, but she does not attend when she is away.

All these developments indicate that Serena is evolving into a critical form of meaning-making. Critical meaning-making is distinguished from pre-critical meaning-making by greater awareness of one's own role in making meaning and by an internalization of authority (what Kegan calls "self-authorship").[25] Serena now recognizes and assumes personal responsibility for meaning-making rather than unwittingly outsourcing her meaning-making to her parents and faith community.

Manifestation in Culture

Serena is a woman of her time in the sense that critical consciousness has come to pervade many Western cultures. Although everyone makes meaning in a pre-critical manner as a child, the culture in much of the Western world has evolved such that it is now common for people to be carried into critical consciousness by the cultural current of a critical mass of friends and family members, popular media, and formal education that all embody critical consciousness. This era of critical consciousness has been called an age of "disenchantment"[26] and "demythologization"[27] as well as the "age of theory."[28]

As a result of various historical developments—including an "excarnation" of Christian religious practices, the advent and subsequent success of the modern scientific method, and the marginalization of God in people's understanding of the workings of the natural world—the old enchanted imaginary through which people once interpreted their experiences came to be supplanted by an "immanent frame," a purely materialistic view of the world. In this disenchanted worldview there is no place for the supernatural.[29] The real is what can be verified by empirical evidence. Where it once would have been perfectly normal to speak about one's experiences using

25. Kegan, *In Over Our Heads*, 185.

26. Taylor, *Secular Age*, 29.

27. Ricoeur, *Symbolism of Evil*, 350.

28. Lonergan, *Method in Theology*, 85.

29. Taylor, *Secular Age*, 221. I refer the reader to Taylor's book for a much more detailed account of these historical developments.

language like "providence," "grace," and "good and evil," people who employ such language in societies that have passed into critical consciousness are increasingly regarded with embarrassment if not derision.

One effect of viewing reality through this sort of critical lens is lowering the community's hopes and expectations for human flourishing from the transcendent and eternal (e.g., heaven) to the merely temporal (e.g., career success, wealth, personal fitness). Cultures imbued with this outlook, which Taylor calls "exclusive humanism," place great value on efficiency, profit, and length of life—values that in many cases conflict with traditional religious values like virtue and the inherent dignity of every human person.[30] Exclusive humanism may be the *de facto* vision even for people who identify as Christian but practically live their lives for worldly aims. As will become clear presently, this nearsighted emphasis on humanity's technical and critical capacities has wrought unforeseen and devastating consequences.

The Breakdown of Critical Meaning-Making

Despite the strengths of critical consciousness, its limitations have become painfully obvious in our own time. If the primary limitation of pre-critical consciousness is lack of logical control over an excess of meaning (i.e., fantastical thinking), the primary limitation of critical consciousness is excessive rationalization resulting in a dearth of meaning. This weakness has become manifest in both the lack of psychological integration experienced by critical meaning-makers and their inability to meet the cognitive demands of postmodern culture.

Although Serena's newly embraced capacity for critical thought is in many respects an advance over her former ways of constructing meaning, at this point in her development, her self-knowledge remains incomplete. As James Fowler explains, critical meaning-makers like Serena are "frequently overconfident in their conscious awareness, [and] attend minimally to unconscious factors that influence their judgments and behavior."[31] For example, they often fail to recognize the extent to which their meaning-making remains indebted to the meanings held within their traditions and communities.

---

30. Taylor, *Secular Age*, 242.
31. Fowler, *Faithful Change*, 63.

Their overconfidence in scientific, critical methods is mirrored by an undervaluation of symbol, story, and ritual. Because Serena perceives her parents' thinking about matters of faith to be muddled and because no one has hitherto been able to satisfy her critical questions about religion, she concludes that all religious belief is naïve. She categorically rejects symbolic, tacit forms of meaning-making as subjective and unreliable and insists that only cold, calculating analysis leads to objective knowing. At first, she feels liberated by sloughing off the religious beliefs and practices of her childhood. However, after she has rejected her religious beliefs and practices and spent some time seeking meaning in secular alternatives like relationships, career, and material success, she finds that she is left with a vague, nagging sense of loss.[32] She cannot with any kind of integrity return to her former beliefs, yet she is haunted all the same by a sense of longing for what she has left behind.

The writings of scientist and philosopher Michael Polanyi help to explain why a critical approach to knowing like Serena's commonly leads to this experience of loss or emptiness. As previously noted, we all yearn for a sense of meaningfulness and coherence in our lives. Polanyi notes that "it is not by looking at things, but by dwelling in them, that we understand their joint meaning."[33] It is symbols, stories, and rituals that best facilitate this sort of in-dwelling and therefore provide the primary means by which we synthesize a holistic view of reality. In taking a relentlessly analytical approach to reality and rejecting religious symbol and ritual, Serena cuts herself off from a fuller knowledge that lies in grasping the whole, not merely its constitutive parts. This is what Polanyi means when he writes that "unbridled lucidity can destroy our understanding of complex matters," in which category the world and a human life are certainly included.[34]

This loss of meaning is ill-timed because twenty-first-century culture has evolved in such a way that an anchoring sense of life's coherence and meaningfulness is needed now more than ever. As a direct result of innovations in technology, communications, and transportation, the world of the twenty-first century has grown so complex that it is now exceedingly difficult for the average person to form a stable worldview or maintain a strong sense of coherence. These developments have given rise to a culture in which we are incapable of performing even a fraction of the cognitive

---

32. Cf. Ozment, *Grace Without God*; Taylor, *Secular Age*, 302–4.

33. Polanyi, *Tacit Dimension*, 18.

34. Polanyi, *Tacit Dimension*, 18.

tasks demanded of us. To quote Robert Kegan, we are "in over our heads" in contemporary society.[35] This is true even for critical meaning-makers, whose analytical mental proclivities are ill-suited to synthesizing a coherent worldview out of the overabundance of fragmentary meanings available in contemporary culture.

These conditions are problematic not only for people's psychological well-being; they are equally problematic for the spiritual life. Christianity was born in a pre-modern context, which offered early Christians a particular set of resources for making sense of their lives and reality as a whole.[36] The "media" that shaped Christians' worldview included the church's liturgy, sermons, the physical environment of the church building, and certain religious practices—all of which remained relatively static for most people's lives. Now, in postmodernity, Christian symbolism is awash in a deluge of pictures, videos, advertisements, and tweets to the tune of two and half quintillion bytes of new data every day.[37] This barrage of media does not bear the clear imprint of any one message or worldview, but the vast majority of it is decidedly not Christian.

Given these circumstances, religious communities' efforts to respond to the constant influx of secular messages in their teachings and communications to the faithful (e.g., papal encyclicals, Sunday school, and even DVD series and YouTube channels) can seem quixotic. Increasing numbers of people are finding a pre-critical Christian worldview incommensurate with their experience of the world in postmodernity. Many who respond by adopting a critical stance toward religion find themselves adrift in an incoherent and overwhelming world.

POST-CRITICAL MEANING-MAKING[38]

Having described critical meaning-making in some depth, it is easy to recognize its manifestations all around us today. Most significantly for the present project, we can now recognize widespread religious disaffiliation and a growing meaning vacuum as predictable consequences of large segments of Western populations moving into a form of consciousness

35. Kegan, *In Over Our Heads*, 9.

36. Cf. Lakeland, *Postmodernity*, 39.

37. Marr, "How Much Data Do We Create Every Day?"

38. Post-critical meaning-making as I describe it here corresponds to Kohlberg's stage six, Fowler's stages five to six, and Kegan's sixth order.

characterized by a critical mindset that rejects symbolic meaning and tacit ways of knowing. I would be quick to add, however, (as are other scholars) that these trends by no means portend an inevitable decline in religious practice.[39] In fact, some of this century's most astute cultural observers have suggested that a further development is already underway. James Fowler asserts that "the present time is a watershed in the evolution of cultural consciousness."[40] Bernard Lonergan, for his part, claims, "The second stage of meaning is vanishing, and a third is about to take its place."[41] Likewise, Robert Kegan has observed that "the distinguishing feature of contemporary culture is that for the first time in human history, three mentalities exist side by side in the adult population . . . the traditional, the modern, and the postmodern."[42]

These scholars and others believe this new development to be a positive one in that a further evolution of consciousness will equip contemporary persons with the capacities needed to overcome many of the mental challenges and social conflicts of the present historical moment. In this vein, Fowler writes, "The construction of . . . postmodern, multiple systemic forms of consciousness represents a practical necessity for reflective persons in our era."[43] Kegan argues that meeting or even understanding the implicit demands of postmodern living requires developing a "fifth-order" consciousness.[44] Educational theorist Jack Mezirow has similarly argued that in order to keep from being overwhelmed by the rapid pace of change and diversity of beliefs that characterize today's world, contemporary adults need to undergo a transformation leading to more inclusive, differentiated, and integrated meaning perspectives.[45]

A number of prominent religious leaders have likewise given voice to the need for contemporary people to become more deliberate in tending to their inner lives. Joseph Ratzinger, striking a cord that would reverberate throughout his papacy, writes in *Truth and Tolerance*:

39. Cf. Casanova, "Rethinking Secularization"; Eisenstadt, "Multiple Modernities."

40. Fowler, *Faithful Change*, 172.

41. Lonergan, *Method in Theology*, 96.

42. Kegan, *In Over Our Heads*, 303–4.

43. Fowler, *Faithful Change*, 174.

44. Kegan, *In Over Our Heads.*

45. Mezirow, *Transformative Dimensions of Adult Learning.* Matthew Geiger, writing about religious education specifically, makes a similar appeal. See Geiger, "Worldview Formation, Reflexivity, and Personhood."

The mystical capacity of the human mind needs to be strengthened again. The capacity to renounce oneself, a greater inner openness, the discipline to withdraw ourselves from noise and from all that presses on our attention, should once more be for all of us goals that we recognize as being among our priorities.[46]

His successor, Pope Francis, has continued in this vein with his frequent writing and speaking on the themes of discernment and maturation of conscience.[47] Even the *Catechism of the Catholic Church* counsels, "This requirement of interiority is all the more necessary as life often distracts us from any reflection, self-examination or introspection."[48] The parallel rise of the mindfulness movement bespeaks widespread recognition within even secular circles of the need for habits or practices that foster self-awareness and centeredness and alleviate the now common experience of being overwhelmed, anxious, and fragmented.

Although these figures employ different terminology and operate within different spheres of thought, they all point to the need for habits of meaning-making that can be aptly described as post-critical. So what defines post-critical consciousness generally? Post-critical meaning-making constitutes a further development in the person's awareness of and control over her meaning-making. Where a critical meaning-makers tends to be overconfident in her own cognitive abilities and unaware of her limitations, the post-critical meaning-maker is more aware of the limits of her knowing and how her bodily experience, feelings and desires, relationships, social setting, and exposure to cultural productions (TV, social media, etc.) all subtly influence the way she thinks and experiences reality. Because she is more aware of these subtle forces, she is better able to modify her own desires and affective responses and to regulate her interactions with others and her consumption of media that she knows are day-by-day shaping her worldview. Part and parcel of this deeper self-awareness is the recognition that the human mind employs intuition and tacit knowing as well as discursive and rational thinking to construct a world of meaning that is more complex than even that person can comprehend. Accordingly, the post-critical meaning-maker comes to recognize her need for ritual and symbolic modes of thought that facilitate psychological integration.

46. Ratzinger, *Truth and Tolerance*, 159.

47. See, e.g., Francis I, "Gaudete and Exsultate."

48. *Catechism of the Catholic Church*, no. 1779.

This point leads to the second respect in which post-critical meaning-making marks an advance beyond critical meaning-making, namely, a recovery of the fullness of meaning. Because of her new appreciation for extra-rational modes of thinking, the post-critical meaning-maker re-appropriates a whole set of tools for making meaning that she had largely abandoned in her critical phase, namely, symbol, story, metaphor, myth, and ritual.[49] This return to symbolic thinking does not involve a regression into naive immediacy or a repudiation of the achievements of critical consciousness. The post-critical meaning-maker does not take the images that arise in her imagination as explanatory but rather understands them as symbolic.[50] Continuing to avail herself of the tools of critical thought, she discovers that it is possible to recover the power and meaning of symbols with all their disclosive possibilities, now through interpretation instead of naive imaginings.[51] In the words of Ricoeur, post-critical meaning-making involves thinking *from* symbols rather than thinking *within* symbols, as was the case in pre-critical meaning-making.[52]

For this reason Ricoeur describes this third phase in the evolution of consciousness as a "willed" or "second naïveté," "the post-critical equivalent of the precritical hierophany."[53] While no longer assuming that her meanings are a *given*, the post-critical meaning-maker may come to recognize meaning as partly a *gift*—not only a gift of her community or tradition but also a gift in the form of divine revelation. In other words, she recognizes her meaning-making as co-constructing meaning in collaboration with a community and a transcendent Source of meaning. She is in this sense at once self-authoring and self-transcending. As a result of this union of the generative powers of symbol and the regulatory controls of critical reasoning, the meaning that she dissected in the critical movement she now reintegrates in a more resilient, more adaptive synthesis.

CONCLUSION

The promise of this chapter was that examining current trends of disaffiliation and loss of meaning on the more granular level of individual

---

49. Cf. Fowler, *Faithful Change*, 15; *Stages of Faith*, 197.

50. See Ricoeur, *Symbolism of Evil*, 350.

51. See Ricoeur, *Symbolism of Evil*, 351.

52. Ricoeur, *Symbolism of Evil*, 355.

53. Ricoeur, *Symbolism of Evil*, 352.

psychological developments would yield a more personal understanding of the obstacles that stand between contemporary persons and the life in abundance that Jesus promises. On the one hand, today's Christians struggle with the same temptations that have always impeded purity of heart and wholeness of life. On the other hand, the experience of Serena and many others like her is radically different from anything Christians (and humans in general) have confronted in the past. The challenge is one resulting from a mismatch between new mental demands emerging in postmodern culture and the meaning-making capacities of the average person. Pre-critical faith consciousness cannot survive without the support of a hospitable Christian culture, the likes of which has rapidly receded in the Western world. The mental tendencies of critical consciousness work counter to the sense of integration and fullness of meaning that make life worth living. It has therefore become necessary for new generations of Christians (or at least a critical mass of them) to develop the capacity to cultivate post-critical habits of Christian imagining.

An allegory may help to illustrate the present situation of Christians like Serena. During her maiden voyage, the young church sailed for a time upon tumultuous waters. Her founder had launched her promising to send favorable winds, and, indeed, after some centuries, the Christian ship had not only weathered the storm but even made safe harbor in a time and culture that proved more hospitable. As more time passed, there built up around her a robust port where she received lavish attention and honor. All that remained to the crew was to scrub the decks from time to time and make an occasional short cruise. In recent years, however, the shore has receded, and the church once again finds herself out to sea. This time she faces not only stormy waters but also enemies who would purge the world of her presence. No longer able to count on the support of a hospitable port, the crew must relearn how to navigate the ship, how to adapt to changing and often unfavorable conditions, and how to make repairs as needed.

No longer able to count on the support of a homogenous Christian culture and confronted by constant criticism and distraction, contemporary Christians must help one another again to see the world through Christian eyes and to keep Jesus' vision of the reign of God alive. In other words, they must evolve to a post-critical form of meaning-making that enables them to regenerate continuously a Christian worldview for themselves. Living well depends upon a vision of life. If contemporary Christians are to enter into the fullness of life that Jesus offers, they must first be able to imagine it.

Up to this point, I have been employing this rather technical language of pre-critical, critical, and post-critical meaning-making (or consciousness) as a means to the end of illuminating the causes underlying our present crisis of faith and meaning. Nevertheless, the reader should not think that post-critical meaning-making is some esoteric theory. The characteristic capacities of post-critical meaning-making—attentiveness to one's psychic needs, the union of critical reasoning and tacit knowing, awareness that meaning-making is always co-authoring—are the means by which significant numbers of people make sense of their experiences every day. In its most basic terms, what I have been describing here is a new deepening of the interiority to which Christianity has always invited its adherents.[54]

When we understand post-critical consciousness in these more basic terms, a recovery of faith and meaning does not seem so impossible. Indeed, I am writing this book because I have witnessed people growing into this new interiority, and I see the possibilities it opens up for them and for our faith communities. The problem is that our faith communities have not yet established the structures, processes, and cultures needed to promote this new form of interiority with any consistency. My hope in this book is to offer a vision of how to change this. In chapters 4 to 6, I will share an approach to religious education that I have found effective in facilitating growth in this new form of interiority.

Before we get to the practical details, however, a couple more foundational questions require our attention: First, it remains to be seen how precisely this new form of interiority relates to the interiority to which Jesus invited his followers and to which Christians of ages past have aspired. Second, we need to clarify how, generally speaking, development to this new form of interiority occurs. Once we have addressed these questions, we will be able to discern more clearly a path to recovering the richness of Christian meaning and the fullness of life in Christ in our postmodern age.

---

54. Cf. *Catechism of the Catholic Church*, no. 1779; Lonergan, *Method in Theology*, 85.

chapter 3

TEACHING FOR CONVERSION TO A NEW WAY OF IMAGINING

In the previous chapter, we drew upon contemporary developmental psychology in order to gain a better understanding of new challenges to meaning-making that have arisen in postmodern societies. We saw that these cultural challenges have made necessary a post-critical form of meaning-making. In identifying this post-critical meaning-making with a new form of interiority, I highlighted the fact that this development in human consciousness has important implications for the faith lives of Christians (and other religious persons). This discovery raises further questions: First, how does this new interiority relate to the kind of interiority that Jesus promoted? Second, how, generally speaking, does development to this new form of interiority occur? Once I have addressed these questions, I will be in better position to describe a pedagogical approach that I have found to be effective in facilitating learners' growth in this new form of interiority.

CONTINUITY FROM THE FOUNDATIONAL INTERIORITY TO THE NEW INTERIORITY

How does this new form of interiority relate to the foundational interiority that Jesus promoted? Most fundamentally, the relationship is one of continuity. All that was essential to the interiority early Christians sought to cultivate remains essential to the new interiority. It will suffice to highlight two key points of continuity. One element that is fundamental to both a foundational interiority and this new form is an active imagination. We have seen how Jesus' parables aimed at upsetting people's established ways of seeing things.

They re-opened and re-activated the imaginations of Jesus' audience that had become hardened and narrow in their vision of who counts as neighbor and who doesn't, who merits salvation and who doesn't, what is righteous and what isn't. An active imagination resists such idolatrous thinking, which results when we grow lethargic in our imagining and become narrowly fixated on our pet principles, doctrines, images, and ways of seeing things. Idolatrous imagining is as much a threat today as it was in Jesus' time, though some of the idols that tempt the postmodern person may be different. If anything, an active imagination is even more necessary in contemporary culture because forming a coherent view of reality has become a never-ending task. Today, we live in an environment where we are assaulted minute-by-minute by billboards, commercials, headlines, and social media updates—all impressing upon our imaginations subtle (and not so subtle) messages about the way things are and how we ought to be.

Another point of continuity between a foundational interiority and this new form is attentiveness to God's presence within us. We saw at the end of chapter 1 how people like Saint Paul, the desert fathers and mothers, and Reformation-era mystics, when facing challenges to faith from the surrounding culture, encouraged Christians to turn to God's presence within in order to renew themselves and the church. In chapter 2, I presented evidence that the need to recover a sense of God's presence in the world and in ourselves has become particularly urgent in the present day. Essential to my proposal in this book (and to Christianity in general) is the conviction that communion with God is indispensable to our human flourishing. A generic form of interiority or "mindfulness" will not suffice. To be sure, the abundance of research on mindfulness now available makes clear how beneficial these practices are for alleviating stress and improving general well-being,[1] but even mindfulness experts acknowledge that mindfulness techniques disconnected from a deeper source of meaning and sense of life's purpose leave practitioners longing for more.[2] Generic meditation practices help to keep the boat afloat amidst the choppy waters of postmodern culture, but a foundational source of meaning is needed to guide the boat towards safe harbors. Christian interiority, as a practice undertaken in response to God's self-revelation, bestows the benefits of generic mindfulness practices while also providing a vision of reality that feeds the human hunger for meaning and purpose.

1. E.g., Bohlmeijer et al., "Effects of Mindfulness-based Stress Reduction Therapy."
2. See Harris, "Yael Shy."

DEVELOPMENT FROM THE FOUNDATIONAL INTERIORITY TO THE NEW INTERIORITY

Although the foundational interiority that Jesus facilitated remains necessary for human flourishing in any age, the challenges of twenty-first-century life have necessitated that Christians develop their inner life in new ways. One of these challenges is living in a radically pluralistic society. In the past, when authority was consolidated in a centralized source like the Catholic Church, it was possible for Christians to more or less unreflectively appropriate a unified worldview by absorbing the teachings of the church and participating in the life of a community built around those teachings. This was Serena's experience before leaving for college and the experience of most Christians until the present century. In contemporary pluralistic cultures, there is no such common authority and Christians frequently encounter people who do not share their beliefs or who actively challenge them. When a pre-critical person's naïve acceptance of the church's authority or of Christian beliefs is challenged—as happened for Serena in college—they are unable both to take these challenges seriously and maintain the meaningfulness of those beliefs. If they are not to simply enter into a bunker mentality, the pre-critical Christian must respond to the new mental challenge by undertaking a critical examination of old beliefs and practices.

Although development to critical consciousness brings real gains, we saw in the previous chapter that this form of meaning-making has proven inadequate to the mental challenges of postmodern culture just as pre-critical meaning-making did in late modernity. While a critical meaning-maker may on one level embrace the radical plurality and the sharpening of thinking that occurs when cultures collide, they lack the ability to synthesize a sense of life's coherence amidst the constant change of globalized society. In sum, the interiority of the pre-critical meaning-maker withers under the scrutiny of critical analysis. The interiority of the critical meaning-maker becomes atrophied on account of their suspicion of ways of thinking, feeling, and imagining that do not conform to the standards of analytical reasoning. The repercussions from the dominance of critical consciousness in modernity have thus made a post-critical recovery of interiority necessary if contemporary persons are again to experience wholeness and deep meaning in their lives.

Such a renewal of interiority involves, on the one hand, a critical awareness of the human mind's susceptibility to fantastical and idolatrous imagining and, on the other, an appreciation of the indispensable role of symbol and symbolic thinking in the life of the human person and in God's communication with human beings. We saw in previous chapters how symbol, story, ritual, and tacit ways of knowing enable us to hold meaning in contexts that defy the analytical mind's efforts to master or systematize the diverse images, messages, and experiences that constitute that context. Re-appropriation of these hallmarks of traditional religion, which the critical meaning-maker had rejected, allows post-critical meaning-makers to find meaning and orient themselves in a complex, rapidly-changing world and in the face of paradox.

James Fowler describes this post-critical recovery in this way:

> They recognize that we have no alternative to embracing interpretations and traditions of interpretation and that the complexity of our situations and demands for knowing commend stances of epistemological humility toward the richness of classic traditions that have perennially been accorded revealed status. From this practical postmodern standpoint it makes sense to eschew relativism, while acknowledging relativity, and with it the necessity of commitment in the midst of an embraced pluralism of such perspectives.[3]

By virtue of their growth into a post-critical form of interiority, these people are able to draw from their religious traditions' deep wells of meaning while remaining open to revising their own meaning frameworks in order to accommodate new information and perspectives, including God's ongoing self-revelation. In this way, the new form of interiority enables them to overcome not only the perennial forces of internal fragmentation (as did the foundational form) but also the new fragmenting forces that characterize twenty-first-century Western culture.

HOW TO EMBRACE THE NEW INTERIORITY —CONVERSION

My aim in the preceding pages has been to demystify the concept of post-critical meaning-making and to cast this psychological development as the latest evolution in Christianity's long history of inviting interior transformation. Recognizing that achievement of post-critical meaning-making constitutes a development in interiority will raise the practical question for religious educators: How does this development to post-critical interiority

3. Fowler, *Faithful Change*, 175.

occur? Put otherwise, why do some people bury their heads in the sand of naïve beliefs while others undergo a radical transformation in the way they make sense of the world?

I believe Ronald Rolheiser points us toward an answer when he writes, "At the end of a long journey towards optimal openness, a journey that ultimately demands conversion in every dimension of our personality, God will spontaneously be part and parcel of our ordinary awareness."[4] This spontaneous awareness of God is precisely what so many Christians and former Christians have lost in the present postmodern age and is precisely what we are trying to recover. Indeed, Rolheiser himself describes this new awareness or consciousness as a "second naivete."[5] As for how to recover this awareness of God, he suggests that conversion is required. This claim affirms what we observed in our discussion of Jesus' teaching in chapter 1, namely, that shaking off our old, narrow ways of seeing things and participating in Jesus' vision of the reign of God means undergoing a total transformation of our imagining and desiring and all of our being. This was true for Jesus' audience, and it remains true for anyone who would follow after him today.

Although entering Jesus' vision of the reign of God always and inescapably involves conversion, that conversion does not look the same in all circumstances. Conversion may occur gradually or, as in the case of Saint Paul, more suddenly. A person can undergo religious conversion within their present form of meaning-making, or conversion may involve transitioning from one form to another. This latter distinction is of particular significance for the present discussion because it means that conversion will look different for someone converting to a foundational form of interiority than for someone converting to the new form.

The transformation Jesus' disciples underwent would have been dramatic. Their lives would have taken on new meaning. However, the cognitive processes by which they made meaning would have in all likelihood remained essentially the same. The culture they lived in was precritical, which meant that no one, whether pagan or Christian, seriously questioned the existence of spiritual beings and their influence in human affairs. In this context, reorienting their thinking and life in order to live in the reign of God did not require critically examining the reasonableness of religious belief. In the present day, by contrast, for someone like

4. Rolheiser, *Shattered Lantern*, 67.

5. Rolheiser, *Shattered Lantern*, 172–77.

Serena to re-appropriate the meaning of the Christian tradition and recover her own interiority often requires making sense of reality in a qualitatively different way. More specifically, it requires both a capacity to check fantastical imaginings that arise in the human mind and an openness to tacit awareness of things (e.g., God's presence) that are inaccessible to analytical thought. These are capacities that we have identified with development to post-critical meaning-making.

It is beneficial for today's religious educators to recognize these different manifestations of conversion because someone converting to a post-critical form of interiority will require different supports than someone undergoing conversion within their current form of meaning-making. Our examination of Jesus' teaching in chapter 1 provided us with a general model for facilitating conversion. In the following section, we will examine how conversion relates to psychological development so as to better understand the nature of the transformation that today's Christians will have to undergo in order to recover a sense of God's presence in the world and within themselves.

CONVERSION AND PSYCHOLOGICAL DEVELOPMENT

In his excellent book *Christian Conversion*, theologian Walter Conn takes up this topic, offering a nuanced treatment of the differences between conversion and development and the interrelation of the two. In the first place, Conn distinguishes conversion from natural psychological development by noting that development is characterized by a predictable pattern of changes leading progressively (if not smoothly) toward the enhancement of certain capacities. By contrast, conversion marks a radical reorientation, turning, or about-face in a person's way of thinking and living. Where development implies continuity, conversion implies disruption.

Of course, development to later stages is not automatic. Some people develop further while others do not. Developmental theorists cannot fully account for these differences in development. We saw in chapter 2 that development to later stages is characterized by progressive self-transcendence, a dying to the old self. We also saw that the human psyche seeks to preserve its internal equilibrium and therefore resists such change. Conn, drawing upon the work of Bernard Lonergan, complements this psychological explanation with a theological one: Left to our own devices, our self-centeredness, biases, and moral impotence impede the self-transcendence that characterizes movement into the later stages of development. We are able to overcome these impediments only by the grace of God. If not everyone progresses to later stages of development, that is because not everyone chooses to accept God's offer of grace, which we need to overcome our inclinations to self-centeredness and self-preservation.

This element of choice, therefore, constitutes another distinguishing feature between conversion and development. People may or (more often) may not be aware that they are undergoing a major developmental change, yet at certain points some sort of conscious decision is necessary for further development. For example, Conn observes that the transition from Kohlberg's conventional to post-conventional moral reasoning involves adopting self-chosen ethical principles, that is, making an intentional decision to be moral rather than uncritically abiding by the rules of one's community.[6] Conn identifies similar decision points in the transitions to Kohlberg's stage six; Fowler's stages four and six; and Kegan's level four. Kegan himself cites religious self-surrender as one medium of the transition from fourth-order to fifth-order consciousness.[7] (It is not incidental that these decision points correspond to the transition points to critical and post-critical consciousness, respectively.) Conn summarizes, "The one transforming process has two dimensions: one unconscious and spontaneous, one conscious and deliberate."[8] The unconscious and spontaneous dimension is that which developmentalists describe as stage transition; the conscious and deliberate dimension pertains to conversion. Developmental stages describe the before and after of the change; conversion describes how the transition happens at crucial developmental moments.

The foregoing makes clear that, although distinct, conversion and development are intimately intertwined. On the one hand, one cannot advance to later stages of development without passing through conversion because of the self-transcendence required. Human beings cannot achieve their full potential—even their potential for psychological development—without undergoing conversion. On the other hand, normal developmental crises sometimes provide the occasion for conversion. As we saw in the previous chapter, development to a new form of meaning-making becomes necessary when the mental demands of a given culture exceed the current mental capacities of people living within that culture. For example, the intellectual

6. Conn, *Christian Conversion*, 110–12.

7. Kegan, *Evolving Self*, 120.

8. Conn, *Christian Conversion*, 129.

challenges of her professors and her encounters with classmates from different cultures prompted Serena's development from pre-critical to critical consciousness. When she was unable to find deep meaning within a critical framework, she felt the need to develop further into a post-critical form of meaning-making. This impetus to further psychological development is also an invitation to conversion, for moving beyond critical consciousness involves admitting the limits of her ability to make meaning and recognizing her dependence on something beyond herself. This recognition may be the prompting that leads Serena to welcome God into her heart.

I have been arguing that Serena's experience is typical of that of many people today. As opposed to the culture of Jesus' day, which was hospitable to pre-critical meaning-making, the rapid pace of change, radical plurality, and irreducible complexity that characterize contemporary US culture overwhelm people who construct meaning at pre-critical and even critical levels. Confronted with their inability to make sense of their reality, such people must make a decision to respond either by clinging to the illusion of control over their lives or by dying to this old self and embracing the role of co-creating meaning with God. This is one significant way that the timeless call to conversion manifests itself in our present postmodern culture. To the extent that religious educators recognize the distinctive manifestation of this decision, they will be better prepared to accompany people through the fraught transition into this new form of interiority.

CONCLUSION

With the conclusion of this chapter, I have put into place the final pieces of the foundation for an imagination-centered approach to religious education that addresses the needs of Christians living in postmodern society. In the first part of the chapter, I explained that current efforts to promote a new form of interiority are, in essence, nothing new to Christianity. From the beginning, Christians have needed to adapt to cultural changes in their efforts to undertake the interior renewal necessary for entering into the life of abundance that Jesus offers. I am by no means alone among my contemporaries in calling for new ways of inviting conversion in response to new cultural challenges. Such has been a constant theme in the writings of the Catholic popes since Pope Paul VI.[9] What is new about the kind of interi-

9. See Paul VI, "Evangelii Nuntiandi"; John Paul II, "Redemptoris Missio"; Benedict XVI, "Verbum Domini"; Francis I, "Evangelii Gaudium."

ority demanded by postmodern culture is the form of meaning-making it entails. As distinct from a more foundational form of interiority, this form of meaning-making includes greater attentiveness to one's psychic needs, the union of critical reasoning and tacit knowing, and the awareness that meaning-making is always co-authoring.

Various religious leaders, educators, and communities have taken varied approaches to addressing the challenges postmodern culture presents to Christian faith and such a diversity of approaches is necessary, for conversion is a holistic endeavor. In the final chapter of the book, I will situate my own project relative to these other efforts and point to areas where further work might be done. For the time being, I merely want to make clear that I do not imagine the pedagogical approach I present here to be some kind of silver bullet.

My more modest aim in the coming chapters is to describe a pedagogical approach or habit that I have found helpful in my efforts to facilitate students' personal (re)integration and recovery of the meaningfulness of life. I believe this approach stands to make a contribution to the work of faith formation in at least two respects: The first is its capacity to extend an attractive invitation to embrace Christian meaning. Attractive invitations are necessary at present because increasing numbers of people in the Western world—young people especially—find Christianity irrelevant, unappealing, even repugnant.[10] We who exercise responsibility within our Christian communities can no longer afford to be complacent or assume that our neighbors—even those sitting in the pews and enrolling for religious education—see the world through Christian eyes and strive to live Christian lives. As the leadership within the Catholic Church has noted, in the current context religious education and catechesis must take on an evangelizing or missionary character.[11] Still, despite dwindling numbers and enthusiasm within American churches, large numbers of students continue to enroll every year in parochial schools, congregational religious education and sacramental preparation programs, and Christian colleges and universities. Their continued presence presents an opportunity for religious educators specifically (as distinct from those working in other areas of church ministry). We need approaches to religious education that

10. Richard Côte offered a similar diagnosis in his 2003 book, *Lazarus! Come Out!* Like Côte, I see the cultivation of the imagination as crucial for addressing people's failure to find meaning in the Christian faith.

11. Cf. Congregation for the Clergy, *General Directory for Catechesis*, no. 33.

recognize this opportunity and are designed to entice and engage citizens of postmodern societies and tap into their distinctive gifts and capacities. What I present in this book is one such approach.

Second, for those who accept the invitation, this approach provides the support and the mental space to respond. Undergoing conversion is always a trying process. Living in a postmodern, critical culture makes it even more difficult, not only because of the anti-religious assumptions ingrained in the culture but also because of the sheer number of impediments to making sense of reality in a coherent way. These challenges demand religious education capable of drawing upon both the timeless wisdom of the Christian tradition and the insights of modern psychology and cognitive science. Only such a blend can provide learners with the support they need to live meaningful lives as disciples of Christ in postmodern culture. These are the concerns that have guided my teaching over the years and shaped the approach I present here.

For all the sophisticated sociological and psychological research underlying this approach, its most basic aim is quite simple, namely, extending an attractive invitation. In my years of teaching learners of all ages, I have found that the most effective religious education does not impose pre-packaged answers or expect passive reception of teachings but rather invites learners to "come and see" for themselves (John 1:39, NRSV). For this reason, I call it the "SEE" approach.

chapter 4

INTRODUCTION TO THE *SEE* APPROACH AND MOVEMENT 1: STIMULATING THE IMAGINATION

From virtually the beginning of my career as a theology teacher, it was clear to me that sharing the faith in a compelling way was going to be a hard sell.

I was volunteering as a parish catechist in college when I got my first taste of what it is like to try to hand on the faith to students who are not eager to receive it. I do not remember much of this experience, nor, I imagine, do my former pupils. No doubt my inexperience was partly to blame for the lackluster catechetical encounter. However, another part of the problem was that I had been plugged into a catechetical model that was not working very well even then. Parents dutifully dropped off their children, who then sat for an hour in school desks listening to an adult lecture from a textbook on morality or the sacraments. There may have been some exercises or art projects mixed in occasionally. It was surely lost on the students how these classes were any different or more important than the lessons they received Monday through Friday in reading, mathematics, and social studies. When I talked to other catechists, it seemed that this was the norm all over.

Nonetheless, I was sure that there was a better way and that I personally was capable of better teaching, so after graduating from college, I signed up with the Alliance for Catholic Education (a sort of Teach for America for Catholic schools). ACE trained me in the competencies of secondary education and baptized me by fire, sending me to teach religion (and several other subjects) at an under-resourced Catholic high school in Memphis, Tennessee. I set out for Memphis prepared to do theological battle with my Bible-thumping Protestant students, but I encountered a different challenge when I actually met them. Most of them did not know enough about their own tradition to know how Baptists and Catholics differed in their beliefs or, for that matter, know enough to care. In general, I met with more apathy than active resistance.

Being a part of ACE, which sends teachers to schools all around the country, gave me a bird's eye view of the state of Catholic education across the nation. For the most part, the view was discouraging—declining enrollment, closing schools, overworked teachers, inadequate resources. I also got a sense for the state of religious education in Catholic schools, which was equally disheartening. In talking with my peers teaching in different places around the country, it seemed that Religion class was in general not taken very seriously. Curricular guidance and standards of excellence were lacking.[1] Too often, it seemed that religious instruction fell to the physical education instructor teaching during his off periods rather than to someone with professional training in the content area.

During doctoral studies and since beginning as a full-time faculty member, I have taught at two different Catholic universities. Despite the fact that the majority of students at these schools identify as Catholic, it has been my experience that many of them are indifferent to religion. Although there are exceptions, many of my Catholic students seem not to have thought very seriously about their faith tradition. They give the impression that it never occurred to them that the teachings of Christianity might be relevant or meaningful for their lives. Although I have rarely encountered students who are antagonistic toward religion, a significant number harbor a dismissive "no one really believes that seriously" attitude.

Through all these teaching experiences, one question had been building in urgency: How can I help my students access the Christian tradition in a way that leads them to discover for themselves its power to transform their lives? At times as a young teacher, I caught glimpses of what was possible. I recall one day in my second year as a high school teacher when I was teaching about Jesus' conflicts with the Pharisees, scribes, and Sadducees. After providing some context and reading one of Jesus' more pithy rejoinders to his Pharisee critics, one of my students, who normally sat slouched in his seat and participated only by lobbing the occasional sarcastic comment, suddenly sat upright and exclaimed, "Yo, that man coooold!" (In other words, that man (i.e., Jesus) is very impressive/interesting/cool.) Something

---

1. There has been some progress since that time, notably with the publication of the US Catholic Bishops' *Doctrinal Elements of a Curriculum Framework.*

I had said led this typically disengaged student into an encounter with the enigmatic figure of Christ. I did not often succeed in replicating this breakthrough moment that year. But, having witnessed my students' faces lighting up on the rare occasion and the wheels turning in their heads, I knew that real transformation could occur in the classroom. How exactly to facilitate such transformative encounters I did not yet fully understand.

HOW I CAME TO *SEE*

In the early days of my teaching career, I tried to answer this question by seeking guidance from other educators, in Scripture, and, when I could sneak it in, the stray book or article. I made some moderate progress toward an answer in this way. Later, when graduate studies and academic appointments afforded me time for more sustained research, I found some pedagogical models that made me feel that I had at last found my way out of the woods and onto the main path. Deeper reading of the Gospels, supplemented by research in biblical scholarship, gave me a fuller appreciation for Jesus' pedagogical genius. As I read his parables in particular, it began to occur to me that there was something more than moralizing going on here, that the parables have an effect on the hearer that goes beyond what can be put into words.

I was fortunate to complete my doctoral studies under the direction of Thomas Groome, whose shared Christian praxis gave me a model of how to bring life to faith and faith to life and an integrating pedagogical framework for the disparate techniques and tips I had cobbled together over the years. Groome's influence on my own pedagogical approach will be very much evident in the following pages, and I will indicate explicitly in various places how the SEE approach relates to shared praxis. Also during graduate studies, I encountered the work of four scholars—Bernard Lonergan, Jack Mezirow, James Fowler, and Robert Kegan—who profoundly influenced my thinking about the challenges of education in the postmodern context and about the kind of education needed to equip learners for life in the postmodern world. These authors helped me to think about learning, including learning about faith, as meaning-making, an insight for which I would later find additional confirmation in the writings of authors like Marcia Baxter Magolda, Sharon Daloz Parks, and James K. A. Smith. In the work of Parks and Smith in particular I recognized projects that were akin to my own and complementary to my more pedagogically-focused response to postmodern challenges to Christian meaning-making.[2]

All the while I continued to teach, applying the research of these scholars in my classroom and observing how my students responded. The results were encouraging. Over time, this praxis of imitating others' teaching, applying educational research, and submitting to the process of trial and error has changed the way I teach. I might even go so far as to say it has changed the kind of teacher I am.

The approach to religious education that I present in this book is the fruit of these years of practice, research, and reflection. In writing this book, I have grappled with how best to characterize this SEE approach. The word "technique" might suggest a tool to be used occasionally and then slipped back into the teacher's tool belt, but this approach demands greater intentionality and discipline. It would not be inappropriate to call it a "process" since its activities follow a distinct pattern, although even this word fails to capture the effect SEE has on the teacher and learners. Therefore, it seems to me that the most appropriate way of describing SEE is as a pedagogical habit.

This terminological point is not incidental to the central argument of this book. In the previous chapter, I argued that for many Christians it is no longer adequate to learn about Christianity or even to learn from it. The mental challenges of postmodern society are too overwhelming and the flood of imaginal influences is too relentless for such a formation to hold up for long. Today's Christians need to develop practices and habits of imagining that will enable them (with God's help) to continuously regenerate a Christian worldview. To state the matter again in figurative terms, the safe shores have receded, and the waters have grown stormy. If the crew is to keep the ship afloat, they must relearn how to navigate her and make repairs as needed.

The requisite habits include attending to the subtleties of our own psychological health, noticing the impact of external influences on our imaginings and meanings, and deliberately refashioning our core mental images. Learning such habits does not happen overnight. Like any habit, these require repetition and practice. It also takes time for another reason. The habits I describe here are incomprehensible to a pre-critical meaning-maker and appear like naiveté to a critical meaning-maker. For this reason, to even begin the journey to a new form of interiority, most

---

2. I will have more to say about the affinities between Smith's and Parks's projects and my own at the end of chapter 7.

people must first encounter a model or mentor who gives credibility to this way of making meaning.[3] They need someone who not only guides and supports them through their transformation but also embodies the new form of interiority towards which they are straining. In this sense, teaching post-critical habits of Christian meaning-making is more like taking on apprentices in a trade than it is like drilling students on dates of church councils. Learners are far more likely to grow in this respect if their teachers practice and embody what they aim to hand on.

Here I must be quick to qualify my claims lest the reader assume only people with doctorates in religious education are competent to employ this approach. In developing the SEE approach, I have kept in mind my experiences of training catechists and religion teachers of varied ages, qualifications, perspectives, and abilities. As I will explain more fully in chapter 7, there are variations and levels of the SEE approach. In its most basic form (namely, following three specific movements in a given teaching experience), the SEE approach is something anyone can do. A teacher need not herself be operating at a post-critical level in order to use it.

In general, I designed SEE to be flexible in its application. I have adapted this approach in a manner that suits my own strengths and style of teaching, and I encourage other teachers to do likewise. It is entirely possible to employ the SEE approach in concert with other pedagogical approaches. In offering this new approach to religious education, I am not suggesting that teachers need to abandon their accustomed methodology. Nor am I proposing an imagination-centered approach in opposition to rigorous instruction in the teachings of the Christian faith.[4] Mastery of core content is indispensable to religious education, and the next chapter will make clear that this is no less true for the SEE approach. I am merely suggesting that, in enhancing their current teaching by attending to the dynamics of learners' imagining (the focus of the SEE approach), religious educators will better prepare their students to make sense of the postmodern world in an authentically Christian way.

---

3. Cf. Taylor on the role of models in undergoing conversion (*Secular Age*, 729). See also Daloz Parks, *Big Questions, Worthy Dreams*.

4. In fact, recent educational scholarship shows that imaginative learning, when done well, actually enhances students' academic performance, even in disciplines like mathematics and physics (Egan et al., *Teaching and Learning Outside the Box*).

OVERVIEW OF THE *SEE* APPROACH

The SEE approach essentially involves three pedagogical habits or "moves." Although a Christian theologian always delights in detecting trinitarian patterns, that is not the reason I have constructed this approach in three movements. In fact, there are several good reasons.[5] To begin with, the reader will recall from the discussion in chapter 1 that human cognition operates according to a distinct pattern: (1) Thought first emerges from sense experience as mental images, (2) then is refined by reasoning and conceptualization, and (3) finally returns to mental images that guide subsequent actions. Secondly, in chapter 1 we observed a threefold pattern in Jesus' teaching that aligns with these dynamics of human cognition, namely, (1) stimulating his audience's imaginations, (2) challenging their accustomed ways of seeing things, and (3) inviting a new way of seeing.[6] Thirdly, in chapter 2 we saw how psychological development passes through at least three distinct forms of consciousness or meaning-making—the pre-critical, critical, and post-critical.

My efforts to follow Jesus' example and to teach in a way that aligns with what this psychological research tells us about how the human mind works have instilled in me three pedagogical habits that have enhanced my effectiveness as a religious educator. These are (1) stimulating the imagination, (2) expanding the imagination, and (3) embracing a new way of imagining.[7] Over time these habits have coalesced into distinct movements within a cohesive approach to religious education. Taking one letter

---

5. To these reasons I might add the industry wisdom that effective communications adhere to the "rule of three." (See Carlson and Shu, "When Three Charms But Four Alarms"; Gallo, "Thomas Jefferson, Steve Jobs, and the Rule of 3.")

6. It is also worth noting the long history of the so called "triplex via" in Christian teaching about God (including in the writings of Pseudo-Dionysus and Thomas Aquinas).

7. After these three movements had become well established in my teaching, I discovered that Robert Kegan identifies three functions—confirmation, contradiction, and continuity—as essential for supporting people in their ongoing work of reconstituting their ways of making meaning. Others have already applied these concepts from Kegan's work to religious education (see Daloz Parks, *Big Questions, Worthy Dreams,* 123; Hess, "Teaching and Learning Comparative Theology with Millennial Students"). For my part, I will draw parallels between the three movements of SEE and Kegan's three functions in each of chapters 4, 5, and 6.

to represent each of the three movements, it seemed fitting to call it the "SEE" approach.[8]

Movement 1—Stimulating the imagination: The purpose of this first movement is to engage learners cognitively and affectively by stimulating activity at the level of their mental images where dramatic, enduring changes in thinking and behavior originate. Key to this movement is presenting images and questions that prompt learners to actively imagine reality as they experience it and encouraging them to give expression to their mental images.

Movement 2—Expanding the imagination: Having activated learners' imagining in Movement 1, Movement 2 aims to challenge their current imagining so as to open them up to ways of imagining that are more authentically Christian and more adequate to the mental challenges of postmodern society. It involves questioning and/or activities that problematize or expose limits in learners' current imagining as well as exploring key symbols, stories, rituals, and teachings from the Christian tradition that potentially offer greater depth of meaning and coherence.

Movement 3—Embracing a new way of imagining: After Movement 2 has disrupted learners' more limited ways of imagining and posed the possibility of more adaptive ways, Movement 3 presents the opportunity and support needed to forge a new, more adequate imaginative synthesis. Key activities in this movement include exercises that promote growth in awareness and control over learners' imagining as well as opportunities to render personal judgments about the adequacy of their orienting symbols and those of the Christian tradition and to make decisions about their lives based on those judgments.

A learning event conducted in accord with this approach may progress through these three movements within a 45-minute class or over the course of a week or even a semester. SEE therefore provides a salutary structure not only for individual lessons but also for the long-term process of facilitating development of learners' meaning-making capacities. For reasons that will become clearer in the final chapter, this approach bears most fruit when conducted in an ongoing manner as opposed to a one-time or occasional learning event. In the remainder of this chapter, I will describe the dynamics of Movement 1. I will describe Movements 2 and 3 and the following chapters.

---

8. The language of "movements" is more appropriate than "steps" since the activities of the different movements frequently overlap and blend with one another and since the process works best when conducted in a recursive fashion.

THE GOAL OF MOVEMENT 1

Like every teacher, I daily face the challenge of getting and holding my students' attention. On a personal level, my desire to engage my students is partly fueled by an aversion to repeating the mistakes of uninspiring teachers I have known. I think in particular of one professor for whom I served as a teaching assistant while in graduate school. The class I TAed, an introductory course on Catholicism, was quite large, with over one hundred students. Due partly to the size of the class and partly to the professor's didactic lecture style, students were generally disengaged. One student was even so bold as to bring a travel neck pillow (such as people use on airplanes) so that he could sleep more comfortably during class time. The professor evidently did not notice or else did not care. Because of that lack of care on the part of both the instructor and the students, no one learned much of enduring value. Certainly no one learned anything that caused them to see reality differently or that changed their lives.

There is much to lament in such a situation. From a purely educational perspective, this professor's style of teaching was unlikely to facilitate meaningful learning. We know from research in the psychology of learning that affective factors like students' motivation and emotional state directly impact how much they learn.[9] Students learn more when they are interested. If the class does not hold their attention, little or no learning will occur.

From an ecclesial perspective, this class was a wasted opportunity. We had a captive audience of over one hundred students, most of whom were Christian. Undoubtedly, a number of "Serenas" were among the crowd—students who were at a crucial transitional period in their development, who were primed to think more critically about the meaning of their lives and about the traditions within which they had grown up, but who also needed support to make sense of a world that was growing more complex by the day. We had an entire semester to explore with them the wisdom and beauty of the Catholic tradition in which they might find the meaning they sought for their lives, but instead, week after week, the professor went through the motions of teaching while the students pretended (barely) to pay attention.

Today many institutions of higher education are recognizing that the complexities of twenty-first-century society demand a different kind of education, and they are raising the standards for teaching accordingly. The church, for its part, has a responsibility far greater than preparing students

---

9. See, e.g., Martinez, *Learning and Cognition.*

for employment or citizenship in today's globalized markets and societies. Its mission is to help people enter into the life of meaning and abundance to which God calls humanity, something that many people are failing to do today. As we saw in previous chapters, meaning cannot be given. The church cannot deposit meaning into people's lives any more than a priest can give people a relationship with Christ by placing a consecrated host in their hands. They must find meaning in the Christian tradition for themselves and weave it into the fabric of their lives. Especially in a time and culture that forces us constantly to make sense of new information and situations, Christian communities need to assist their members in deliberately taking up the work of constructing meaning in concert with the received tradition. Of course, people will only seek meaning in the Christian tradition if they feel that it will be worth their while, that is, if it somehow attracts their attention.

A beginning is a precious thing that ought not be wasted. This is particularly true when it comes to teaching, especially in a time when the margin of error for capturing students' attention has grown so small. This lack of attention and interest poses a significant obstacle to transforming learners' meaning frameworks. Religious educators are not alone in their search for methods that will engage learners more actively. Transformative, engaged, mindful, and contemplative pedagogies are all founded on the understanding that gaining learners' attention and recruiting their active involvement leads to more profound learning.[10] Despite their different methods, all of these approaches seek to effect a shift from conceptual, "crystallized" thinking to "fluid," exploratory thinking,[11] or, in the words of Jack Mezirow, to "reactivate the intentionality implicit in perception."[12] Since conversion to the reign of God implies radical change in a person's thinking, the SEE approach likewise aims to free learners of their ossified categories and reactivate their active imagining.

My own experience as a teacher has confirmed what these authors write about the importance of activating learners' thinking at the outset. Driven by an aversion to meaningless class time and the recognition that so many Christians today are disengaged from their own tradition, I have always been intentional about planning the first part of a lesson or

10. See Mezirow, *Transformative Dimensions of Adult Learning*; hooks, *Teaching Critical Thinking*; Langer, *Power of Mindful Learning*; Barbezat and Bush, *Contemplative Practices in Higher Education*, respectively.

11. Feuerstein et al., *Changing Minds and Brains*, 149.

12. Mezirow, *Transformative Dimensions of Adult Learning*, 22.

presentation in a way that would engage my students and immerse them in their own experiences. When I have done this, my efforts have been rewarded by better energy in the classroom and by students offering more interesting comments and questions. By contrast, when I have skipped this part of a lesson or rushed it, the lesson was more likely to fall flat. In time I would come to recognize the fruit these preliminary activities were bearing not just in that moment but also later in the learning process. In this way, these habits were solidified as the first indispensable movement of what would become the SEE approach.

GENERATING INTEREST WITH IMAGES

By now it should be abundantly clear why it is so important to recruit students' active engagement at the beginning of a learning event. There are myriad advantages to doing so using images, particularly images that are comprehensible, interesting, and meaningful to the learner.

To begin with, taking an image as the point of departure for a learning event coheres with the natural dynamics of human cognition. Thomas Aquinas long ago observed that "nothing is in the intellect that was not previously in sense" and that mental images provide the crucial connection between the senses and the intellect, claims that have found support in the contemporary research we examined in chapter 1.[13] For this reason, images exert a stronger pull on our attention than words, and we understand more quickly and remember better when we are able to associate the concept or idea in question with an image.[14] The primacy of the imagination also becomes apparent when we consider how human beings develop across a lifetime. In the beginning, children are overwhelmingly concrete, image-focused thinkers. More abstract modes of thought only emerge and mature in the adolescent and young adult years. This pattern of development makes an image-centered approach like SEE suitable for both children, who struggle with abstraction, and adults, whose thinking remains rooted in images even after they have developed this capacity for abstract thought.

A second reason for starting from images is that images elicit emotion (much more so than concepts), and emotion contributes to resilient learning. A child quickly learns her lesson about touching a pot of boiling water

13. Aquinas, *De Veritate*, q.2, a.3, arg.19.

14. For a fascinating and entertaining exploration of the relation between memory and mental imagery, see Foer, *Moonwalking with Einstein*.

on the stovetop. She needs no reminding because of the fear attached to the painful memory of the first time she made that mistake. More positively, learners find new ideas and information more meaningful and interesting when they relate to their personal passions as, for example, in the case of an aspiring astronaut studying the planets in science class. Both of these examples involve images (a burning pot, the planets) that elicit emotion. Engaging learners on an emotional level becomes even more important when the goal is not just adding to their store of knowledge but inviting a conversion in their imagining. Emotion is crucial for conversion because a person must desire conversion (eventually if not initially) in order for it to come to fulfillment. Given this crucial role of affectivity in learning, a learning experience that begins from affect-laden images is more likely to lead to meaningful growth.

One feeling that is particularly important for meaningful learning is the feeling of security. When we feel uncomfortable or threatened, the cognitive processes necessary for learning shut down.[15] For example, a pre-critical meaning-maker (think of Serena in her first days at college) might respond to a professor's historical-critical interpretation of Scripture by dismissing it as the idle speculations of an ivory tower academic. A critical meaning-maker (like Serena after graduation) might feel insecure and defensive while talking with a religious colleague who seems to be leading a happier, more fulfilled life. Whatever learners' developmental level, teachers need to help them overcome their feelings of discomfort and achieve some sense of security in order to coax open the blossom of their mind. Robert Kegan refers to this affirming of learners' needs, limits, and current ways of making meaning as "confirmation."[16] One way of offering confirmation is by starting the learning event with something familiar to learners. Because of the primacy of the imagination in human cognition, images are inherently more familiar and comfortable than concepts and arguments. When a teacher presents learners with familiar images, they generally evoke positive feelings and put learners in a more relaxed, open state.

Jesus' teaching illustrates this point well. Images of everyday life abound in Jesus' parables—a lost coin, baking flour, wineskins, fishing nets, household servants, wedding feasts. He frequently evoked the objects and events of the natural world that constituted the background of quotidian life in first-century Galilee and Judea. He described the natural beauty of

15. See chapter 6 of Sharot, *Influential Mind.*

16. Kegan, *Evolving Self,* 258.

flowers, birds who neither sow nor reap, and seeds that sprout into plants. Some scholars have even suggested that, while telling stories, Jesus took cues from his immediate setting in order to add to their realism.[17] Jesus also drew liberally from the imagery of the Hebrew Scriptures—for example, vineyards, sheep and shepherds—images with which his mostly Jewish audience would have been intimately familiar. As such, Jesus' audiences would have felt very much at home when he began telling a story. (The end of the story is a different matter, as we will see in the next chapter.)

FOCUSING THE IMAGINATION

The aforementioned research and Jesus' pedagogical example both point to the benefits of beginning the learning event with what Thomas Groome calls a "focusing activity," an activity that activates learners' memories, mental images, interests, questions, and concerns as they relate to a particular "generative theme" or "symbol."[18] A teacher might choose from many types of focusing activities, including a story, a painting, a movie, a poem, or a field trip. Regardless of the type of activity, the most effective focusing activities are those that evoke some interesting and personally meaningful image in the mind of learners.

The generative theme or symbol need not be explicitly religious (although it might be), but it is crucial to the effectiveness of the lesson that the teacher selects a generative focus that bears a strong connection to the material to be presented in Movement 2. As Groome explains, an effective generative focus "signals to participants . . . the vital core of the curriculum to be attended to throughout this whole event."[19] In the words of Catechesis of the Good Shepherd innovator Sophia Cavalletti, it should give learners "in a flash, the global intuition of the essence of the subject we are considering."[20] Selecting an appropriate generative symbol is important because, if teachers employ an image that is interesting but loosely related to the Christian symbol in focus, learners may remember the image or

17. For example, James Martin describes arriving at the so called "Bay of Parables" on the shore of the Sea of Galilee and finding himself standing upon terrain marked by rocky ground, fertile ground, and even a thorn bush—precisely what Jesus described in the parable of the sower (Matt 13:1–23; Mark 4:1–34; Luke 8:4–18) (Martin, *Jesus*, 198).

18. Groome, *Sharing Faith*, 155, 156.

19. Groome, *Sharing Faith*, 156.

20. Cavalletti, *Religious Potential of the Child*, 98.

story but miss the point of the lesson (an experience many of us have had when it comes to homilies and sermons).

Having followed the lead of Jesus and Groome in my own teaching, I can testify to the effectiveness of this approach. One of the most powerful lessons I have taught to undergraduates over the years is a lesson on the Incarnation. I believe the key to its effectiveness is in its beginning. I start the class by showing the music video for Vance Joy's song "Mess Is Mine."[21] The video follows a figure in a polar bear costume on a nocturnal journey through urban streets inhabited by a variety of strange characters. It is a bizarre video that generates feelings of chaos. Because of the strangeness of the video's images (and because of the catchiness of the song), students are always rapt in attention. The video evokes positive feelings because it is a popular song with which most students are familiar, but it also evokes curiosity. At this point in the lesson, many of them are wondering why they are watching such a strange video in their theology class.

Provoking such curiosity is precisely my aim in beginning class with this video. When I have the opportunity to teach theology to undergraduate students, most often it is in the context of required introductory-level courses. Many students do not want to be there and do not enter the classroom with particularly open minds. A good number come from Christian backgrounds and assume that this class will simply rehash the same material to which they were subjected throughout their childhood religious education. Others have already developed a suspicion of religion and written off theology as a useless, unscientific discipline. Recognizing these various layers of resistance, I find it essential to break down students' mental barriers and reopen their imaginations at the outset of a lesson.

Given young people's love of music, music videos are a great tool for stimulating their imaginations. However, religious educators have many other tools at their disposal. For her part, religious educator Mary Hess uses commercials as prompts for theological reflection in her classes as well as in church settings.[22] Vibrant Faith, an organization that provides training and resources for faith formation, has recently undertaken a new initiative they are calling the "Visual Faith Project."[23] Grounded in research in current brain

---

21. Joy, "Mess Is Mine."

22. Hess provides links to some of her favorites on her Storying Faith website: http://www.storyingfaith.org/archives/780.

23. Information about the Visual Faith Project is available at https://vibrantfaith.org/visualfaith.

science, their approach begins by inviting participants to select from a pile of attractive photographs (or from images on their iPhone app) one that seems most interesting to them. A facilitator then poses a variety of questions about God, self, and others that lead into an engagement with Scripture. More low-tech options also abound. Teachers might present an image using a paper handout, by telling a story, or by leading learners in a guided imaginative meditation. Alternatively, students might perform a skit or act out a scene from Scripture, as in the "Bibliodrama" approach.[24] Teachers can also ask questions that prompt learners to generate their own mental images. Regardless of how the teacher presents the image, the most effective images will be those that are vivid and easily reproduced in learners' minds.

Since the purpose of the focusing activity is to engage learners on the level of their everyday imagining and living, teachers should conduct this preliminary activity in a way that taps into reality as learners know and experience it and makes them feel at home in the learning event.[25] As suggested above, images drawn from quotidian experiences and popular culture tend to be most effective in this regard. During the focusing activity, it is generally best to avoid abstract, technical language that would take learners out of an imaginative mode of thinking or cause them to tune out.

GETTING PERSONAL

I have been stressing the value of utilizing images that are familiar to learners. I find that when I begin a learning event from an image that relates to my students' lives, it naturally leads them to reflect on their personal experiences. Making the lesson personal in some way is crucial for learning that is meaningful to students. Therefore, another key to the effectiveness of Movement 1 of the SEE approach is prompting learners to actively imagine reality *as they experience it* and encouraging them to give expression to their mental images in their own terms (not in those they think the teacher wants to hear).

On a basic pedagogical level, activating students' prior understanding and experiences is considered an educational best practice because research

---

24. Pitzele, *Scripture Windows*.

25. Teachers will find two superb models of this approach in the writings of C. S. Lewis (e.g., *Mere Christianity*) and Rob Bell (e.g., *Velvet Elvis*; see also Bell's Nooma video series at https://www.youtube.com/user/NOOMAtube).

has demonstrated that it improves learning and retention.[26] On a deeper level, recruiting students' active involvement becomes particularly important when pursuing a more ambitious learning objective such as the one at which SEE ultimately aims, namely, facilitating a conversion of learners' imaginations to a post-critical form of meaning-making. Educational theorist and practitioner Marcia Baxter Magolda's Learning Partnerships Model aspires to the related goal of promoting students' self-authorship, which she defines as the capacity "to internally define [one's] own beliefs, identity, and relationships."[27] Among the principles that Baxter Magolda has found to be essential for promoting self-authorship are (1) validating learners' capacity to know and (2) situating learning in learners' experience, both of which are fulfilled when a teacher begins a lesson with an invitation to give expression to and examine personal images.[28]

There is another reason for beginning a learning event this way that is more specific to the concerns of this book. Today many young people dismiss religion as irrelevant to their lives.[29] Of course, it has always been necessary to integrate faith and life. It would seem Jesus was attempting to do just that in describing the reign of God using activities, objects, and settings from his original audience's everyday lives. Today's audiences, however, are not as disposed to recognize the presence of the divine in the world as were Jesus' contemporaries. Where generations past took for granted that their religious devotion would make them better people and bring them blessings in this life and the next, newer generations do not necessarily see why religion is essential for their well-being.[30] Those who know the Christian tradition well know that it speaks fundamentally to our human condition. It is not that Christianity lacks relevance. However, changing cultural circumstances now make it necessary for religious educators to be more intentional about helping others see the connection between faith and life. For that reason, I believe it is worthwhile to highlight this task as a key to the success of the SEE approach.

Now how concretely to make the lesson personal? It is crucial to shift the cognitive burden from the teacher to the learners. Rather than focusing on the teacher and what she is presenting, learners now focus on the

26. See, e.g., Ambrose et al., *How Learning Works*.

27. Baxter Magolda, *Making Their Own Way*, xvi.

28. Baxter Magolda and King, *Learning Partnerships*.

29. Pew Research Center, "US Public Becoming Less Religious."

30. McCarty and Vitek, *Going, Going, Gone*, 12.

memories, images, and visions the focusing activity has stirred up within them. Learners are best able to make this shift when the teacher explicitly provides them with an opportunity to identify and give expression to some aspect of their current imagining.

Teachers can prompt this transition in a variety of ways. Most simply, the teacher might ask learners a question or series of questions or invite them into conversation around the focusing image. The conversation might even take the form of learners sharing personal stories that relate to the focusing image. Or, rather than telling stories, learners might work together in groups to create and perform skits that express the way they collectively imagine and think about the topic at hand. Alternatively, learners might engage in an art project wherein they give expression to their imagining through traditional mediums like paper, paint, and clay or using digital media like Prezi,[31] Animoto,[32] and Glogster.[33] In her book *The Grace of Playing*, Courtney Goto describes how one congregation focused its members' collective attention by installing a life-sized tree in the worship space and then inviting members to help "grow" the tree by adding leaves with personal notes about what each person was willing to do to promote change at the church.[34] For learners who are less imaginative or have a harder time articulating their mental images, choosing a preferred image from among two or more options can be helpful (e.g., Do you see society more as a wild jungle or one big family?).

Here is how I shift the cognitive burden to students in the Incarnation lesson I started describing above: After showing the Vance Joy music video, I share a brief anecdote about a friend who is constantly spilling her coffee, losing her keys, arriving late, and generally leaving a wake of disorder behind her. I ask the class if anyone knows someone like this, and everyone raises a hand. I add that, even if we are not all quite that much of a mess (although some in the room might be), we all have our moments when we feel that our lives are a total mess. I then invite students to discuss in pairs the messiness of their lives and of the world they live in (school stress, broken relationships, terrorism, the environmental crisis, etc.). I encourage them to be concrete and describe a time when they or someone they know was in a real mess. (Giving the option provides them with an emotional buffer.)

31. https://prezi.com.
32. https://animoto.com.
33. https://edu.glogster.com.
34. Goto, *Grace of Playing*, 87.

This is a topic on which everyone has something to say, and students are quickly engrossed in conversation.

In this part of the learning event, the ideal is to activate learners' core symbols of God, self, and world. This opening salvo of my Incarnation lesson activates students' thinking around their images of self and world, bringing into relief the aspects of these images that reflect the world's and their own brokenness. (We get to their God-image in Movement 2.) Although every lesson need not focus on these master symbols, it is important to engage them regularly since they constitute the nucleus of our worldview. Undergoing conversion necessarily involves the transformation of these most basic building blocks of meaning in our lives.

From time to time, it is beneficial for learners to give expression to their symbol system as a whole. The beginning and end of a course are particularly appropriate occasions. Such exercises of "metacognition" (i.e., thinking about their own thinking) help learners to promote skills like regulating attention, monitoring their own learning and meaning-making, and maintaining a positive outlook in the face of intellectual obstacles.[35] These are all skills that we have identified as necessary for leading faithful, meaningful lives in the postmodern world. Thinking about their symbol systems can also help learners to integrate their imagining, a point I will address more fully in the chapter on Movement 3.

Concept mapping is one proven technique that learners can use to express their symbol systems.[36] On paper or their electronic devices (touch screens with drawing features work well) students sketch or label their master images as they imagine them (e.g., God as King or Mother, self as middle child or star athlete, world as their oyster or a battlefield) and map out their relationship to other personally significant symbols (e.g., place of worship, heroes, enemies, primary community, objects of desire). Teachers can then lead students in reflecting on why they imagine their core symbols as they do, how they relate to other symbols that are prominent in their lives, and the significance of all the above.

Teachers may occasionally find that a student is at a loss when it comes to this activity. This should not come as a surprise in light of what we have said about the widespread loss of meaning in postmodern culture. Given these cultural circumstances, it is entirely possible—even likely—that some of our students will lack a coherent symbol system or way of imagining their

35. Wilson and Conyers, *Teaching Students to Drive Their Brains.*

36. Heinze-Fry and Novak, "Concept Mapping Brings Long-term Movement."

life experiences. Especially during the college and early adult years, many young people find themselves in a situation similar to Serena's where, after a class with an iconoclastic professor or after taking a job in a new part of the country, their old worldview has been torn down and they are simply trying to rebuild. In such cases, teachers should encourage learners to represent their imagining as is—with gaps and missing connections—rather than imposing a contrived order. The important thing at this early stage of the process is to peel back some of learners' protective outer layers and expose their living, flowing imaginations. To attempt to impose meaning, especially at this sensitive stage, is to risk triggering learners' natural psychological defenses, thereby closing the door on any meaningful change.

RAISING QUESTIONS

Already hinted at in the preceding sections is the crucial role of questions in opening up learners' imaginations. As Groome points out, a truly generative theme or symbol always presents a question to participants.[37] When learners encounter some symbol that evokes an expansive theme like identity, purpose, suffering, or redemption, they sense there is something here that merits a closer look. Implicitly (and sometimes explicitly) they wonder, "How does my life reflect this reality? Is there some important wisdom here? Is this theme inviting me to some kind of change?" Recognizing the power of such "big questions," Sharon Daloz Parks highlights hospitality to questions as one of the key ways that mentoring communities support young adults in recomposing meaning and faith.[38]

Questions of this kind also give direction to the learning process. In one sense, learners' own imaginations must be the driving force behind their conversion to a new way of constructing meaning. A worldview develops most organically when growing from the inside out. Still, the imagination is a wild spirit that sometimes requires a guiding hand. That guiding hand must also be gentle. Overly didactic methods can send the imagination running into hiding, but a good question can coax the imagination out and lead it to open pastures. Questions are naturally enticing. Their open-endedness invites exploration. When posed in a genuine spirit of inquiry, they encourage construction of new meaning by giving us a bit of material to work upon and the direction and the mental space to do so.

37. Groome, *Sharing Faith*, 182.
38. Daloz Parks, *Big Questions, Worthy Dreams*.

Asking good questions is a skill that commonly sets apart master teachers like Jesus. Jesus had a way of both capitalizing upon his audience's questions, using the occasion to draw them into a vision of the reign of God, and posing his own questions to prompt new ways of imagining. He asked his audience about the meaning of the Law (Matt 12:11; 15:3; Mark 7:18; Luke 10:26) and how they understood the Scriptures (Mark 9:12; John 5:47). He asked about who is worthy of love (Matt 5:46), who counts as family (Matt 12:48), what constitutes true wealth (Matt 16:26), what makes someone great (Luke 22:27), and about the details of their everyday lives (Matt 6:27–28; 7:16; Mark 4:21; Luke 15:8). Such questions prompted Jesus' hearers to look past facile labels and ingrained assumptions. They threw his hearers back on themselves and reopened issues they had long regarded as settled matters.

As for more contemporary examples, the process set forth in the Visual Faith Project uses well-crafted questions to channel the imaginative energy generated by attractive photographs towards an encounter with Scripture. Questions like, "Why is [this image] amazing to you?"; "What words would you put to this image?"; and "Where do you see God at work in each image?" nudge participants to articulate what is flowing through their imaginations and prepare them to receive the Word of God with a thoughtful, inquisitive disposition.[39] In her guide to theological reflection, Mary Hess presents similar questions aimed at evoking personal images or encouraging exploration of those images after participants have viewed a generative commercial: "What is existence like within this image? What is lifegiving and joy-filled about it? What is broken or sorrowing about it? What possibilities for healing and newness exist within it?"[40]

Going back to my lesson in the Incarnation, after students have had the opportunity to call to mind a time when they were in a real mess, I follow up by asking them to think about how others tried to comfort them in the midst of their suffering. I ask them to discuss what they found helpful and what was less helpful. There is often some variety in their responses, but the majority tend to converge upon the conclusion that simply offering a sympathetic presence is most helpful. These questions and the discussion they draw out set us up for Movement 2 of the lesson in which I frame the

---

39. Questions cited from the Visual Faith Bible app.

40. Hess's guide to theological reflection can be downloaded from http://www.story-ingfaith.org/archives/780.

Incarnation as God responding to the mess humans had made of the world by entering into that mess alongside us.

Movement 2 will later afford time for more focused, clarifying questions. However, at this point in the learning event, the most effective questions are those that turn learners to their own experiences and imaginings. Mindful of where the lesson is heading, a skilled teacher will ask questions that anticipate a central theme from the Christian tradition without being too heavy handed. Students can sense the difference between when teachers are asking earnest, exploratory questions and when they are asking with the "acceptable" answer already in mind. Given the high value today's young people place on authenticity, teachers risk alienating learners from the start by posing questions in a way that seems disingenuous or manipulative.[41] The goal at this time is not so much to provide content as to till the soil of their lives, memories, and imaginations. When teachers and learners take the time to prepare the soil in this way, the seeds of wisdom the teacher later brings forth from the tradition are much more likely to take root and eventually bear fruit in students' lives. Welcoming learners' own questions as Jesus did is also helpful in this regard.

The teacher needs to be sensitive as to how deep to till at this stage.[42] For younger students or students the teacher is still getting to know, it is best to stick with questions that simply invite students to share about their lives and imaginings. The questions cited above from the Visual Faith app and Mary Hess's guide are good examples of this kind of question. For older students with whom the teacher has established a certain level of trust, it is possible to ask questions that probe deeper, questions about the origins and context of learners' experiences and images. For example: Where do you think your image of success comes from? How has growing up in a wealthy nation like the United States influenced your self-image? Do other people have different ideas about what is necessary for a happy life? Such questions invite learners to examine their assumptions and images more critically, anticipating the disruption that is to come in Movement 2.

41. Cf. Moore, "Authenticity."

42. When the aim is promoting psychological development and even more so when aiming for conversion, as is the case with the SEE approach, it is imperative to take learners' developmental levels and readiness into account. Challenging learners who are not cognitively or emotionally capable of coping with the challenge can result in setbacks and obstacles to future growth. On the other hand, failing to challenge learners who are ready deprives them of opportunities to grow.

A PEDAGOGICAL TEMPTATION

It can be tempting to rush through this first movement of the SEE process or to skip it altogether when facing pressure to cover a prescribed amount of material. Some educators, lacking awareness of the relevant findings in educational research, regard preliminary activities of this sort as "fluff" and prefer to get right to the "real substance." As a result of such pressures and misunderstandings, learning exercises like those described above are the most likely to be cut from lesson plans and skipped over in textbooks. This is a mistake, for teachers who neglect to activate learners' thinking, questioning, and imagining at the outset will find themselves stymied later.

Of course, in making this prediction, I am presuming that the teacher is aiming for a more transformative kind of learning. It is entirely possible to cram facts and definitions into students' heads without troubling to generate interest in the topic, but this kind of teaching seldom if ever leads to real change in the ways people make sense of and live their lives. Present cultural circumstances demand a more transformative approach to faith formation, and truly transformative learning does not happen without considerable preparation on the part of the teacher and willing participation on the part of the learner.[43] Tempting as it might be to dispense with this first movement of the process, teachers who invest the time up front to till the soil will find that their students reap a richer harvest later on.

HABITS OF A NEW INTERIORITY CULTIVATED IN MOVEMENT 1

Preparing learners to live meaningful lives of discipleship in postmodern society requires more than simply giving them meaning prepackaged in definitions and doctrines. It requires facilitating their growth in a new form of interiority, which is to say new habits of imagining that will enable them to construct meaning in whatever circumstances they find themselves. To borrow a common analogy, it means teaching them to fish for a lifetime rather than feeding them for a day. Although the most sophisticated aspects of this formation will occur in Movements 2 and 3 of the SEE approach,

---

43. Maria Harris's classic *Teaching and Religious Imagination* offers a wonderful model of careful preparation for transformative learning and a compelling testimony to the benefits of such preparation.

crucial habits are already being cultivated in Movement 1. These are, in large part, habits of attention and anticipation.

Much depends on how and what we anticipate. We do not simply see what there is to be seen; we anticipate what we will likely see, which then affects what we actually perceive. The mind also fills in what the senses do not provide. A man does not have to look up from the dinner he is preparing to know who is walking through the door. He knows by the time of evening and the way the door opens that it is his wife. So crucial are our habits of expectation for the way we make meaning that Mezirow can claim they constitute a person's orienting frame of reference.[44]

The design of the SEE approach reflects the importance of our habitual expectations. To begin with, Movement 1 habituates learners to expect something new when they enter the learning space. Adult learners especially tend to have their world divided into neat categories and their minds made up about matters like religion. However, by learning to engage each lesson with the imagination as well as the intellect, SEE participants develop more fluid habits of thinking. Like the people listening to Jesus' parables, they learn to expect that all labels and categories will prove insufficient sooner or later and that they will see reality more clearly when they keep an open, active mind. In this sense, Movement 1 embodies what Ellen Langer calls a "mindful" approach to learning and bestows many of the same benefits.[45]

As rigid mental categories break down, learners become more attentive to how those categories are formed, that is, to their own meaning-making. This often happens naturally, but I find that it helps to draw learners' attention explicitly to the ways they construct meaning. One way I have done this is by guiding them through a meditation on how they make sense of their experiences by attending to the data of the senses and consciousness, asking questions about that data, formulating answers to those questions, and judging the accuracy of those answers.[46] I ask them a sequence of questions that includes the following: Do you hear my voice right now? Are you paying attention to my voice instead of other noises in the background? (Attending) Do you ever ask questions like, "What is this

44. Mezirow, *Transformative Dimensions of Adult Learning*, 42.

45. Langer defines mindful learning as that which involves "the continuous creation of new categories; openness to new information; and an implicit awareness of more than one perspective" (Langer, *Power of Mindful Learning*, 4).

46. I based this exercise on Lonergan's account of human cognitive operations in his *Insight*.

exercises about?" (Questioning) Do you seek answers to your questions when they arise? Do you sometimes have an "ah-ha" moment when you figure out the answer? (Understanding) Do you wonder if your ideas are right? Do you make judgments about their accuracy based on evidence? (Judging) I often conduct this exercise with my first-year students at the start of the semester and thereafter regularly draw their attention back to the workings of their own minds.

Besides helping learners to attend more carefully to their own experiences and meaning-making, Movement 1 habituates them to anticipate finding something meaningful and relevant in their encounters with the Christian tradition (and elsewhere). As suggested above, this is not the habitual expectation of many young people today. On account of their previous experience, many of my undergraduate students show up to their first-year theology course expecting a thoughtless rehearsal of Catholic doctrine or a semester-long indulgence in pious fantasies untethered in reality. Because we human beings tend to find what we are looking for (and miss what we are not looking for), an important first step towards finding meaning in the Christian tradition involves questioning assumptions and entrenched habits of thinking. In fact, I do find that over the course of the semester a change occurs in many of my students. Week after week, they have the experience of being surprised, puzzled, or intrigued and of being thrown back on their own experiences and seeing themselves in the texts we read. As a result, they come to expect that, when we approach some text, artwork, or ritual from the Christian tradition in this class (and, I hope, outside of class as well), they will find something relevant for their lives. They become conditioned such that their anticipation of engaging the tradition begins to stimulate automatically memories, questions, and the workings of their imaginations.

For example, it is common for my Catholic students to tell me that they have never read the Bible the way we read it in class. Many of them are used to hearing the Scriptures read during Sunday worship in a monotone and homilies about the Scriptures that float upon clouds of abstraction, never touching down upon the ground of daily life. Furthermore, they live in a culture where the "immanent frame" has for many become the default worldview. Looking at reality through this lens, they do not expect to encounter the divine or the transcendent. Theirs is a flattened world. In our class, by contrast, they read the Scriptures as texts that address the existential questions burning in their own minds. They come to see themselves in the figures of Adam and Eve, Abraham and Sarah, Peter, and Mary Magdalene. Having spent some time imaginatively immersed in the world of the Christian Scriptures, their view of the "real" world begins to take on a similar hue. The key difference between their previous experiences of reading Scripture and their experience in class is that, before we open the text, I have cued them into their own experiences and questions that parallel those in the reading.

Changing habitual expectations in this way is the first step in someone like Serena reconsidering the Christian tradition (or considering it seriously for the first time). Only if learners approach the tradition with an open mind and active imaginations will they find therein the sort of meaning that can reinvigorate their lives. This habitual openness and expectation is thus one of the habits of imagining that characterizes the new form of interiority.

CONCLUSION

In this chapter I have begun to describe how I developed a set of pedagogical habits that eventually coalesced as the SEE approach. The first cluster of habits described above all serve in one way or another to stimulate learners' imagining, that is, to till the soil of their imaginations in preparation for a transformative encounter with the symbols, stories, and rituals of the Christian tradition. We saw above why the habit of beginning a teaching event in this way is conducive to transformative learning (and learning in general). For one thing, it coheres with the natural dynamics of human cognition in which thought first emerges in mental images. For another, starting this way puts learners at ease and opens them to new ways of imagining. As learners grow accustomed to beginning learning events in this way, they develop a habitual expectation of learning something new and meaningful for their lives.

That is all well and good, the reader might be thinking at this point, but there does not seem to be much that is innovative about this first movement of the SEE process. Much of what has been described above merely reflects current best practices in education. I do not dispute the point. The most innovative elements of SEE, the elements that most directly facilitate conversion to a post-critical form of meaning-making, are found in Movements 2 and 3 and in how the process works as a whole. Notwithstanding, the methods of these later movements presuppose of the learners a certain degree of mental engagement, openness, and awareness of their own imaginings. Without these, Movements 2 and 3 tend to be far less effective. Movement 1 may not seem particularly innovative, but it is essential.

As we move on into chapters 5 and 6, we will see how the three movements of SEE both mirror psychological development from pre-critical to critical and then post-critical meaning-making and work together to facilitate learners' progression through this developmental process. Movement 1 mirrors pre-critical meaning-making insofar as its activities operate largely within the realm of the imagination, not yet pushing learners to apply critical reasoning to their imaginings. It contributes to the development process by opening the learner's imagination, the engine behind meaning construction, in preparation for receiving, reshaping, and constructing new meanings in Movements 2 and 3. This preliminary step is particularly important for critical meaning-makers whose imaginations have atrophied or stagnated because they have favored a narrow understanding of the rational faculties. It is helpful for pre-critical meaning-makers as well, though they generally require less coaxing to engage Christian symbols, stories, and rituals than do critical meaning-makers.

Regardless of learners' developmental level, stimulating the imagination is a necessary step on the journey towards a new form of interiority. When they begin to question long-held assumptions, when the imagination awakens and again begins to roam, then they are ready to undergo an expansion of their imaginations. To this development we now turn.

chapter 5

MOVEMENT 2: EXPANDING THE IMAGINATION

The goal of Movement 1 was to spur learners' imaginations into action. Opening up the imagination in this way, we saw, is a necessary preparation before learners will consent to undergo a major change in the way they construct meaning. Because we tend to resist new meanings when we feel insecure or threatened, opening up learners' imaginations requires engaging what is familiar and comfortable to them and establishing some level of trust. It requires, in Kegan's terminology, "confirmation."

As teachers, it is tempting to stick to ideas and activities that are comfortable and that foster good feelings, but we do our students a disservice when we push no further. An experience from my days as a high school teacher illustrates why. In my first year at the high school, the principal charged me with planning and directing the senior retreat. For several months, we met regularly with the student leaders, worked with them on their witness talks, and laid our plans. When the weekend of the retreat finally arrived, things seemed to go well. The students opened up to one another and bonded more tightly as a class. The tone of the retreat was positive, and everyone enjoyed themselves. At the welcome back ceremony, students gushed about how great the retreat had been. However, when the adult chaperones met to debrief the following week, it became clear that the retreat had not really succeeded. As one chaperone pointed out, not a single student had mentioned God at the welcome back ceremony. The retreat had affirmed the students, their experiences, and their relationships with one another, but it had not challenged them to enter more deeply into relationship with God or to strive for something greater in their lives.

It is easy to fall short in the same way in the classroom, and I often have. Because of my desire not to repeat pedagogical mistakes like those I witnessed as a teaching assistant, I was overly concerned as a first-time teacher with my students' affective responses to my teaching. I wanted them to be engaged and interested, and I evaluated my effectiveness as a teacher in large part based upon how much fun my students seemed to be having. It was a rude awakening when I started grading the first round of exams and discovered that many of my students may have been enjoying class but were not learning much. I learned the hard way that facilitating meaningful learning requires not only capturing students' interest but also challenging them to take on the unfamiliar and uncomfortable.

This is particularly true when it comes to teaching the faith to young people today. The wider culture does not, on the whole, support a Christian worldview. Indeed, the currents of modern media often seem to flow very much in the face of a Christian way of life. Faced with these circumstances, it is utterly inadequate merely to affirm learners in where they already stand with regard to their outlook on faith and life. If they are not actively moving ahead, they will soon drown in the swirling eddies and vortexes of post-modern culture. As teachers of the faith, we need to challenge learners not only to develop an authentically Christian worldview but also to strengthen their capacity to confront this countervailing current as it continues to grow stronger. The exercises of Movement 2 represent my efforts to challenge learners to grow in this way.

GOALS OF MOVEMENT 2

In order for such growth—for such an expansion of the imagination—to occur, two things must happen: First, learners must recognize the limitations of their current ways of imagining. Growing into a new form of meaning-making is unlike acquiring new information in that it is not sufficient to build upon an existing foundation. Because embeddedness in one form of meaning-making prevents making meaning in a different way, the old machinery must be dismantled in order to get the new model up and running. The exercises of Movement 2 thus confront learners directly with the limitations of their accustomed ways of constructing meaning and, consequently, with the need to change.

Second, learners must be able to see a way forward through the transition. Inevitably that vision will not be perfectly clear because a crisis of meaning is precisely the inability to make sense of what one is experiencing. Nonetheless, if learners can at least catch a glimpse of a more adequate worldview and way of imagining, they will have found a life raft in which to weather the storm until they can find a sturdier vessel. It is the responsibility of teachers of the faith to provide learners with this life raft in the interim. In the SEE approach, this support primarily takes the form of giving learners access to meaning-full, life-giving symbols and coaching them in how to build new meaning around those symbols.

Exposing the limits of accustomed ways of constructing meaning and proposing more adequate ways are thus the two primary tasks or goals of Movement 2. Although I distinguish these two tasks for the sake of clarity, in actuality they often occur simultaneously during the learning event. They are, in other words, two dimensions of the one process of expanding the imagination. This second movement of the SEE process pushes learners beyond the familiar and comfortable, beyond the world bounded by their own narrow desires and limited capacity to make sense of reality, in order to draw them deeper into relationship with God and the reality of God's ongoing creation.

EXPOSING INADEQUATE IMAGINING[1]

When I first began teaching high school, I had the benefit of a summer's worth of education classes, so I knew that effective teaching required getting students to construct knowledge actively rather than merely pouring information into their heads. That being said, I did not yet fully appreciate the obstacles that students' prior beliefs and convictions could pose to new learning. Another anecdote will help to illustrate my point. One day in my second year of teaching high school, the topic of homosexuality came up in my freshman religion class. Aware of the strong views on homosexuality of many people in this community, I was careful to present the Catholic Church's teaching clearly while also attempting to foster in my students greater understanding, compassion, and respect for members of the LGBT community. When at one point I mentioned that experts believe that sexual

---

1. As stated in chapter 2, a person's manner of constructing meaning does not make them morally superior or inferior. However, different forms of meaning-making can be more or less adequate to the demands of a given context. It is in this limited sense that I employ the language of "inadequate" with regard to the relative adequacy of pre-critical and critical forms of meaning-making to the postmodern context.

orientation is influenced partly by genetics, one student objected vehemently. I responded by presenting the student with the findings of various scientific studies, which he rejected out of hand. Although I was not surprised to encounter strong reactions to this topic, I was flummoxed by the student's refusal to listen to reason and scientific evidence.

Years later, further psychological research would make it clear to me that my inability to change this student's mind was not an isolated incident. Studies consistently reveal that we more readily absorb information that confirms our existing views and dismiss or gloss over information that contradicts them.[2] For this reason, evidence and arguments are generally ineffective at prompting change in people's view of the world. Naturally, reading this research made me wonder why some people do change their minds.

As it turns out, psychological research corroborates something that anyone who wears corrective lenses already knows. As a negligent wearer of glasses, I am sometimes oblivious to how dirty my glasses are. I do not notice the accumulating filth because I rarely look at my glasses or contact lenses. Usually I am looking through them at other things. Often it is only when my lenses begin to irritate my eyes that I realize how dirty they have gotten. Even though not everyone wears glasses or contacts, we all see the world through a particular set of "lenses" generated by the workings of our minds. Just like a contact lens wearer, we typically only recognize the need to clean or change our imaginative lenses when they begin to irritate, that is, when our accustomed way of seeing things becomes problematic.

Many leading figures in modern educational theory have recognized that a crisis of meaning typically precedes significant changes in meaning and meaning-making. Paulo Freire, in his classic *Pedagogy of the Oppressed,* explains that in order for learners to gain a critical awareness of their own existential situations (i.e., undergo "conscientization"), the teacher must reflect back to learners their view of the world in "problematized" terms.[3] In *The Transforming Moment,* James Loder similarly describes "conflict," a rupture in the knowing context, as the first step in the knowing event that leads to a transformed perception, perspective, or worldview.[4] Jack Mezirow has likewise found that learners typically need to go through a "disorienting dilemma" before they are willing to undergo a change in their meaning

---

2. Sharot, *Influential Mind.*

3. Freire, *Pedagogy of the Oppressed,* 90.

4. Loder, *Transforming Moment,* 31.

perspectives.[5] Robert Kegan, while emphasizing the need for "confirmation" of learners' ways of constructing meaning, also insists on the necessity of "contradiction" in helping them to develop more adequate ways.[6]

The consensus of these educational authorities on this point persuaded me of the need to challenge my students' assumptions and accustomed ways of seeing things. As I incorporated these methods—tentatively at first and then more regularly—I only grew more convinced of their necessity and effectiveness. In what follows, I describe how this disruptive pedagogy has taken shape within the SEE approach.

Disrupting Inadequate Imagining Through Self-Examination

As we will see shortly, serious engagement with the symbols at the heart of Christianity can itself challenge our accustomed ways of seeing things. Notwithstanding, I have found that at times it is more pedagogically effective to invite learners to examine their personal experiences, assumptions, and imaginings before explicitly introducing Christian content into the discussion. This may be prudent, for example, when teaching learners who find Christianity uninteresting and are not initially disposed to engage the tradition seriously.

Such has sometimes been the case with my students who grew up in a homogenous Christian community or culture and therefore had never questioned their Christian worldview. For such students, appropriating the Christian tradition in a more intentional and meaningful way requires complicating the way they make sense of reality. Insofar as Movement 2 of the SEE approach invites learners to examine their imaginings more critically, it mirrors and facilitates the natural course of human development from pre-critical to critical meaning-making. That being said, it has been my experience that, given current cultural circumstances, critical meaning-makers are often the ones who stand to benefit the most from such self-examination. In the case of such students, the crucial task is to disrupt their excessive self-assurance and flattened view of reality rather than complicating naïve religious thinking.

There are many ways of prompting a crisis of meaning that leads to critical self-examination. In chapter 2, we saw how people can enter into a crisis of meaning when they encounter people who are different from

5. Mezirow, *Transformative Dimensions of Adult Learning*, 148.

6. Kegan, *Evolving Self*, 258.

themselves, for example, when leaving home to attend college like Serena. Teachers can capitalize upon these natural encounters with otherness in the classroom setting by asking questions that draw out students' differing viewpoints.[7] A particularly dramatic encounter of this sort occurred in my classroom on November 9, 2016, the day after Donald Trump was elected to the presidency. I knew that many of my students would be troubled by the result of the election, and I felt it important to provide a safe space for talking about it. After reminding students of the ground rules for open and respectful conversation we had observed all semester, I opened the floor for conversation. The students' comments reflected a variety of perspectives and reactions. Some clearly had a hard time understanding how some of their peers could think or feel the way they did about the new president-elect. I had not planned this discussion in advance, and my first priority in that moment was helping students to process their experience of this divisive election. Still, this conversation had the unintended effect of prompting students to examine their personal assumptions as a prelude to engaging Pope Benedict XVI's *Deus Caritas Est* (the assigned reading for the day) and discussing the demands of self-giving love.

Of course, disruptions do not always naturally arise in a way that aligns with the teacher's lesson plans. In situations where the student body is relatively homogenous or certain perspectives are underrepresented, teachers can welcome guest speakers into the classroom, either physically or virtually. Telling stories, reading literature, and viewing news reports and other modern media about different people, cultures, and customs can also be effective means of disruption. Direct experience is even more effective to this end, a fact that may be partly responsible for the current popularity of service-learning programs.[8] Personal encounters with impoverished persons, immigrants, refugees, or victims of racial discrimination can shake up complacent thinking as few other things can.

Entering into such discussions or encounters, students begin to question assumptions and worldviews they had previously taken for granted. I have often found it beneficial to help students along by articulating challenging questions explicitly in a way that gives them pause to examine their own lives. In this regard, I echo Sharon Parks's emphasis on the importance

---

7. Cf. the disruptive role of "communities of discourse" in Mezirow, *Transformative Dimensions*, 212.

8. On the effectiveness of service-learning in facilitating meaningful learning, see Eyler et al., *Where's the Learning in Service-Learning*.

of asking the big questions. Parks writes, "Since faith is the dynamic composing of meaning in the most comprehensive dimensions . . . [questions] reveal the gaps in our knowledge, in our social arrangements, in our ambitions and aspirations."[9] The big questions Parks has in mind include, "Who do I really want to become?"; "What are the values and limitations of my culture?"; and "What is my religion? Do I need one?"[10] For the purposes of facilitating a conversion of the imagination, the best questions are those that cause learners to reflect on their accustomed manner of imagining: Have you ever considered looking at the matter differently? Why do other people see things differently? How did you come to see things this way? What effect do these images have on your relationships, behavior, and values? What would your life be like if you imagined things otherwise? What are the advantages and disadvantages of imagining in this way?

How deep the teacher presses with these questions will depend upon learners' psychological and emotional readiness.[11] Teachers cannot push very young students much in this regard because they lack the life experience necessary for questions of this depth to be meaningful. Furthermore, when teacher and students are still getting to know each other, it typically takes some time for students to gain the level of trust with the teacher and one another needed to probe these questions honestly and openly. However, for older students with whom the teacher has established a certain level of trust, it is possible to ask questions that probe deeper into the origins and context of learners' experiences and images.

Sometimes a disruption occurs naturally within the learning event, as happened for my class the day after election day. Sometimes teachers have to engineer one. At other times, however—and this is increasingly the case—students arrive in our classrooms and churches already in a state of crisis. The conditions of today's pluralistic, media-saturated culture constantly disrupt our efforts to form a consistent, coherent vision of reality. The best many of us can do is snap up disparate tokens of meaning like a vagabond rifling through dumpsters in search of a day's worth of sustenance.[12] When working

9. Daloz Parks, *Big Questions, Worthy Dreams*, 137.

10. Daloz Parks, *Big Questions, Worthy Dreams*, 137.

11. I do not have the space here to go into detail with regard to what kinds of questions and activities are appropriate for different age groups. I refer readers to works like Kegan's *The Evolving Self* and *In Over Our Heads*, which present markers whereby educators can track learners' developmental progress as well as guidelines for the kinds of support needed at different moments in the development process.

12. Cf. Miller, *Consuming Religion*.

with learners for whom this is the case, it may serve pedagogically simply to draw their attention to this lack of meaning or coherence in their lives. The above-mentioned lesson on the Incarnation illustrates this approach. Many of my students readily identify with the experience of life as a mess and of struggling to make sense of it all. Simply inviting them to discuss the messiness of their lives suffices to generate awareness of what they lack and to tap into their desire for something more meaningful.

Drawing Learners into an Encounter with the Christian Tradition

As a Christian educator, I teach out of the Christian tradition because I believe it can lead others to the fullness of life we all seek. My hope for my students is that they will engage the tradition seriously, that they will step inside it and roam around. I am confident of the riches they will find there once they do. The challenge is getting them through the threshold. In the previous chapter, I described how working to overcome students' apathy and preconceptions led me to cultivate the pedagogical habits that I came to associate with Movement 1 of the SEE approach. However, the challenge arises again when it comes time to shift learners' attention from their own experiences to the stories, symbols, and visions of the Christian tradition. As in Movement 1, I find that the key is to keep the learning event focused on images. As a teacher and presenter, time and again I see the difference this makes in my audiences. When I stop lecturing and start telling a story or unpacking a symbol, they stop shifting in their seats, they lean forward, a light enters their eyes. Images draw them in.

Walter Brueggemann has written, "The deep places in our lives—places of resistance and embrace—are not ultimately reached by instruction. Those places of resistance and embrace are reached only by stories, by images, metaphors and phrases that line out the world differently."[13] Brueggemann's observation gives us an insight into why Jesus preferred to teach in stories and images and, more generally, why God chose to reveal Godself not only in words but also in history and in visible signs.[14] The most significant of these signs is, of course, Jesus himself, who, taking on human form and dwelling among us, has manifested the glory of the invisible God (Col 1:15; John 1:14).

13. Brueggemann, *Finally Comes the Poet*, 109–10.
14. Cf. Paul VI, "Dei Verbum," no. 2.

In the Catholic tradition in particular, there is an understanding that certain symbols are not "merely" symbolic but actually cause what they symbolize. The Catholic Church applies this language most often to the seven sacraments, but it also applies more broadly to the revealed symbols at the heart of the Christian faith. It is in this sense appropriate to describe Jesus as the primary symbol or sacrament of God's salvation to the world.[15] For Jesus not only represents God's love and salvation; he actually brings it about. The way Jesus as a symbol transforms our imagining, our way of seeing reality, is part of that work of salvation.[16]

Still, there are many today who do not see the transformative, life-giving potential of Christianity. In their eyes, Christianity is an institution that binds its adherents with many restrictive rules and doctrines. Of course, those who have committed their lives to following Jesus know that there is more to the Christian faith than that. In sentiments that he would later echo as pope, Joseph Ratzinger soundly rebuffed such a superficial view of Christianity, declaring, "Christianity is not an intellectual system, a collection of dogmas, or moralism. Christianity is instead an encounter, a love story; it is an event."[17] The reason people are not finding meaning in Christianity is not that there is no meaning to be found there. The more likely reason is that Christians have failed to communicate that meaning effectively. If that is indeed part of the problem (and I believe it is), then it seems prudent to renew our efforts to share God with others the way God has shared Godself—in experience, story, and symbol.[18]

In his momentous book *The Analogical Imagination*, David Tracy proposes precisely this sort of approach to doing public theology in a pluralistic society. Tracy writes with sensitivity to the mindset of postmodern people who, influenced as they are by living in a critical culture, are little inclined to accept anything on authority or tradition. Such people are more often compelled by empirical, existential verification.[19] Recognizing this cultural reality, Tracy pins his hopes for the future of public theology on what he calls Christian "classics"—symbols, images, texts, events, and persons that

---

15. Cf. Schillebeeckx, *Christ the Sacrament of the Encounter with God.*

16. For an in-depth discussion of how specific images mediate God's transforming grace to human beings, see Doran, *Theology and the Dialectics of History*, 286–91.

17. Ratzinger, "Funeral Homily for Msgr. Luigi Giussani"; cf. Benedict XVI, "Deus Caritas Est," no. 1.

18. Cf. Côte, *Lazarus! Come Out!*

19. Cf. McCarty and Vitek, *Going, Going, Gone*, 24.

bear an excess of meaning.[20] The attractiveness of Tracy's approach lies in the fact that one need not believe that these classics are divinely revealed in order to find something of value in them.[21] As religious classics, the core symbols of the Christian faith—particularly Jesus Christ—have the capacity to capture our attention, illuminate our experiences, and give coherence to our imagining and living. They possess a power that goes beyond that of the typical TV commercial or YouTube video, which attracts our attention but offers nothing more than what appears on the surface. Christian classics inspire fascination and awe because we sense that a deeper—perhaps inexhaustible—meaning lies within.

True to Tracy's promise, religious and theological educators have found in these classic Christian symbols a powerful means of drawing contemporary people into the tradition and enriching the meaning in their lives. Paul Lakeland's *The Wounded Angel* confirms and complements Tracy's theory by offering personal reflections on the author's experience of teaching classic works of literature. I, too, have experienced the power these classic Christian texts exert, even for otherwise disengaged undergraduate students. Year after year, I am surprised by the way that the Book of Genesis, Augustine's *Confessions*, and Dante's *Divine Comedy* stimulate students' imaginations and open up new existential possibilities for them. As a teacher, it is a joy to teach these classic texts. It is also something of a relief knowing that the burden of engaging students is not entirely on me, for the texts have their own life and appeal. As for the students, engaging these texts often proves to be a transformative encounter. The writings of authors like Brueggemann and Tracy and the experience of teachers like Lakeland and myself thus suggest that centering Christian religious education around classic, revealed symbols may be our best bet for transforming and integrating postmodern learners' imaginations.

Of course, not every symbol bears classic or revealed status. This fact lays great weight on the pedagogical decision of which symbols to focus on in the learning event. Although it is appropriate that teachers should have some discretion in how we organize and teach our classes, our selection of Christian symbols should not be arbitrary or a medley of personal favorites.

20. Tracy, *Analogical Imagination*, 108.

21. Canadian psychoanalyst Jordan Peterson's approach to interpreting the Bible is a perfect example. The remarkable popularity of his lectures on the Bible, which have been viewed millions of times, demonstrates that many people continue to find deep meaning for their lives in the Bible, even if they do not read it as sacred Scripture. See, for example, Peterson, "Biblical Series I."

Rather, we should look to incorporate the symbols in which the Christian community has through the ages consistently experienced God's grace and illumination. Reflection upon the history of God's dealings with human beings has over the millennia yielded an enduring story, albeit one with many sub-plots and told by a diversity of voices. God's self-revelation to humanity has also yielded a symbol system that, like the constellations of the night sky, has reliably guided the lives of generations of Christians while always allowing for the emergence of new meanings and new initiatives of the Spirit. The North Star of that symbol system and of the Christian imaginary is the controlling symbol of Jesus Christ. Whatever the preferred hermeneutic and the generative symbols for a particular teacher or community, these must consistently refer back to Jesus and his vision of the reign of God, which for Christians norm the interpretation of those other symbols.[22] Without this primary reference point, all other symbols lose their proper meaning and run the risk of becoming idols unto themselves.

While Jesus' central importance should be obvious to all Christian educators, it is sometimes less clear what are the other classic, revealed symbols around which we should build our lessons and presentations. Such was the case for me and many other teachers I know in our first years as catechists and religion teachers. When I began my first full-time teaching assignment the administration gave me a textbook that I could not possibly cover in a semester's time and left it to me, an inexperienced teacher, to decide what was important to cover and what to skip. This sort of situation is entirely avoidable because the church does offer guidance in this regard.[23] It is crucially important that schools and church communities communicate this guidance to their teachers.

The *locus classicus* for the core teachings of the Catholic Christian faith is the Creed, also referred to since its inception as the "symbol" of

22. Of course, other religious traditions will interpret these symbols differently. For example, although Muslims do not believe that Jesus is divine, they honor him as an important prophet. Similarly, the symbol of the Kingdom of God (or Heaven) continues to have relevance in Judaism independently of Jesus' use of this symbol. These varying interpretations of these symbols exemplify what Tracy means when he argues that a classic can provide rich meaning for diverse audiences, even those who do not attribute them revealed status.

23. The specifics of that guidance will, of course, vary among the various Christian and religious traditions. Catholic educators like myself will find a source of guidance in magisterial documents like the *General Directory for Catechesis* (see especially no. 130), the US Bishops' *Doctrinal Elements of a Curriculum Framework*, and, most authoritatively, the Creed as discussed in the following paragraph.

faith. Both the Nicene-Constantinopolitan and Apostles' forms of the Creed expand upon the symbols of God the Father, Jesus the Son, the Holy Spirit, the church, sin, and resurrection from the dead using biblical as well as philosophical language.[24] Implicit in the text is the three-part story of salvation history—creation, redemption, and sanctification. These are the central symbols that Christians have discerned through reflection, prayer, worship, and lived experience to be revealed by God for our salvation. Therefore, these are the symbols that should form the core of all Christian religious education.

As the central symbols of the Christian faith, these encompass and relate to many other revealed symbols. The general symbol of creation evokes (among others) the more specific symbols of God as Father, Mother, and Creator as well as the narrative of Genesis 1–2 and the symbols contained therein (e.g., the first man and woman, the garden, the tree of life). Concerning sin and the Fall, prominent symbols include those in the narratives of Genesis 3–4 (e.g., the tree of knowledge of good and evil, expulsion from Eden, the first murder), Satan, Israel's idolatry, the sins of Israel's kings, and hell. Concerning redemption, prominent symbols include those found in the gospels and epistles, particularly Jesus' birth/Incarnation, parables, miracles, death on the cross, resurrection, and ascension. For reasons noted in chapter 1, Jesus' parables are uniquely efficacious for the purpose of converting imaginations to the reign of God and therefore deserve a privileged place in Christian religious education. Key symbols concerning sanctification include the Holy Spirit, the liturgy and sacraments, the church, apostles, disciples, saints, and heaven. Each of these symbols has the power to illuminate and bestow new meaning upon our experiences. However, it bears repeating that these symbols derive their meaningfulness and coherence from their relation to the controlling symbol of Jesus and his vision of the reign of God.

While following the guidance of the universal church, teachers should also select symbols with a sensitivity to the needs, culture, and resources of the local community. Symbols can carry different meanings and connotations in different communities and cultures. In some places certain symbols are central to the identity of the people within that community; in other places less so. For example, a teacher working with a Mexican population would be making an egregious error by failing to incorporate

---

24. Less frequently used today is the Athanasian Creed, which never gained acceptance by Eastern Christian churches.

the symbol of Our Lady of Guadalupe into their reflections on faith.[25] Symbols that are evocative of womanhood and motherhood, like Mary and feminine images of God, will naturally resonate with women.[26] Sharon Parks suggests that images of truth, transformation, self, other, and interrelatedness are vital for young adults in particular as they learn to envision more meaningful lives for themselves.[27]

As noted above, Tracy's definition of a classic includes not only symbols and texts but also persons. Clearly the person of Jesus Christ is *the* religious classic for Christians. Although the various Christian denominations differ in the degree to which they honor the saints, Tracy's notion could also extend to them. Speaking as a Catholic educator, I can testify to the impact of the lives of holy men and women like Dorothy Day and Thomas Merton on my students. The stories of the saints reveal in flesh in blood, in the real circumstances of everyday life, what it looks like to live into Jesus' vision of the fullness of life. My students are fascinated by and attracted to Day, who writes so joyfully (but also realistically) about life in the Catholic Worker communities, and Merton, who sets before them an inspiring vision of what a university education could and should be.[28] They also encounter these classic figures as oddities and as a challenge with their countercultural views of what constitutes success and a good life. Because of their concreteness, variety, and narrative quality, the lives of the saints exert a tremendous force of attraction, particularly when we do not gloss over their struggles and imperfections.

Practically speaking, selecting the Christian symbol or symbols that will serve as the focal point of the learning event is typically the first step in the SEE planning process. Everything else flows from this focal symbol. Once teachers have made a selection, they can then plan out the Movement 1 activities that will lead to exploration of those symbols in Movement 2 and the Movement 3 activities that will follow upon this exploration. If the teacher is following a textbook or established curriculum and the lesson topics are predetermined, the teacher's role is to bring into relief the symbols inherent in those topics. For example, at the heart of a lesson on

---

25. Hosffman Ospino's book *El Credo* offers one model of how to relate Our Lady of Guadalupe to central Christian beliefs for a Latino audience.

26. See Cassidy and O'Connell, *She Who Imagines.*

27. Daloz Parks, *Big Questions, Worthy Dreams,* 148–54.

28. In my course for first-year students, we read Day's *The Long Loneliness* and Merton's piece "Learning to Live."

salvation stands the cross. At the heart of a lesson on the church reside images such as the Body of Christ or the People of God. Approaching these topics as classic symbols rather than merely as doctrines helps learners to recognize them as invitations to deeper meaning.

Disrupting Inadequate Imagining Through Encounters with Christian Symbols

Classic Christian symbols not only fascinate, they also disturb. A closer examination of Jesus and his parables will reveal why.

In the previous chapter, we examined the effectiveness of Jesus' parables in connecting with the familiar, everyday elements of his audiences' lives. However, anyone who listened to Jesus for long quickly found themselves in unfamiliar territory. It is evident that many found this irritating. His Jewish audiences had clear ideas about who was friend and who was foe, and they found it irritating when Jesus intimated that an odious Samaritan could be a good neighbor. They were surely also irritated by the unorthodoxy and inconsistency of Jesus' parables. He likened God and God's reign to many different things, some of which (e.g., yeast, a mustard seed, an unjust judge) held decidedly negative connotations for his first-century Jewish audience.

To elaborate on just one of these examples, in the parable of the mustard seed we see Jesus pivoting upon a familiar, comfortable image into a decidedly discomforting vision. Jesus describes the mustard seed growing into a large shrub or vegetable with large branches in which "the birds of the air can make nests in its shade" (Mark 4:32, NRSV). This phrase is likely an illusion to Hebrew Scriptures (e.g., Ps 104; Ezek 31; Dan 4) in which it is usually a mighty cedar tree (a symbol evocative of Israel's hopes for restored greatness) giving shade to birds and animals. However, Jesus has unexpectedly substituted the cedar tree with the mustard vegetable, an invasive plant that carried ambivalent connotations for his Jewish audience. This substitution would have had the effect of shaking up the facile categories of his audience, prompting them to think afresh about what God's reign is like.

Jesus also had a habit of developing a theme in one parable only to overturn it in the next. We see such a reversal in the fifteenth chapter of Luke's Gospel. There, Jesus tells two parables (the parables of the lost sheep and lost coin) in which the protagonists search diligently for what they have lost. When Jesus then begins to tell a third parable of loss, the audience expects the father to go out in search of his lost son. Their expectation is frustrated, however, when the father allows his son to go off into a life of dissolution and waits in idle hope for his return.[29]

The regularity with which Jesus' parables exploded accepted categories, reversed expectations he himself created, and generally confused his audience suggests that he intentionally sought to confound their accustomed way of seeing things. In the words of Walter Conn, "It is the parable's precise design and purpose to shake the foundations of our safe and comfortable world of convention."[30]

Jesus provoked his audiences not only by telling parables but also by virtue of his very manner of being. He ate with people with whom he was not supposed to eat. He violated laws his contemporary Jews considered inviolable. He cared not for the things that dominated their thinking. William Lynch seems to touch upon the truth when he writes, "If Christ is the most central image of faith he is also the most bothersome image of faith."[31] Even for us today, Jesus of Nazareth disrupts many of our categories and expectations: In his person, God manifests Godself, not in power and might, but in humility and weakness. Through this one man, who lived in a particular time and a particular place, people of every nation and every age receive the offer of salvation. Perhaps most shockingly of all, it is Jesus' ignominious death that restores the possibility of life for God's children. Part of what makes other Christian symbols classics is that they, too, disturb us. The thought that (in the Catholic understanding) when we receive the Eucharist we are eating Jesus' body and drinking his blood scandalizes our imaginations, or at least it should. The utter lack of concern for human regard by saints like Francis of Assisi embarrasses us profoundly.

That these Christian symbols so grate upon our imaginations reveals to us how distorted human imaginations have become. If we lack meaning and direction in life, that is perhaps because we have set our sights upon idols with no power to save rather than on the one true God. Saint Paul describes humanity's folly in this way: "Claiming to be wise, they became fools; and they exchanged the glory of the immortal God for images resembling a mortal human being or birds or four-footed animals or reptiles" (Rom 1:22–23; cf. 2 Cor 4:4). Because our imagining has become so distorted, Jesus' disruption of our imaginations is a necessary step in our

---

29. Levine, *Short Stories by Jesus*, 45.

30. Conn, *Christian Conversion*, 213.

31. Lynch, *Images of Faith*, 96.

conversion. Our images of God, self, and other are too small to accommodate the fullness of the reality to which Jesus invites us. In order to enter into Jesus' vision of the reign of God, we must suffer a disruption of all we think we know, acknowledge the inadequacy of our images, and recognize our dependence upon God for a life full of meaning.

Contemporary researchers in psychology and education indirectly highlight the genius of Jesus' disruptive pedagogy. One such group are researchers of "conceptual change," a field that seeks to understand how to overcome misconceived knowledge. A significant insight to emerge from this body of research is the remarkable effectiveness of image-centered interventions for correcting inaccurate or unhelpful thinking.[32] One proven strategy involves correcting scientific misconceptions by comparing flawed visual representations (e.g., of the solar system) with accurate ones. Although theology clearly pertains to a different kind of knowing, such techniques can also be effective in theological and religious education. For example, a teacher might contrast a holy person like Oscar Romero or Dorothy Day with a modern celebrity to raise the question of what it looks like to live life fully, or contrast celebrating the Eucharist with Netflix binging as an alternative vision of what truly nourishes the soul.

I attempt to do something similar in my lesson on the Incarnation. As described above, I begin the lesson by showing a music video that dramatizes the messiness of life. In the second movement of the lesson, I use PowerPoint to present another series of images of messiness, namely, Jesus' birth in a stable, his passion, and his crucifixion. As students behold these images, I draw out their significance in the Christian tradition and for our discussion of suffering: How does God respond to the mess that human beings have made of the world? According to the Christian account, God does not leave us to wallow in our misery, nor does God fix things from a safe distance. Rather, God in the person of Jesus takes on a human body and enters directly into the mess of human suffering. Seen in this light, these images prompt students to reexamine their assumptions about the struggles of being human and how best to deal with them.

To offer another example, a teacher might invite learners into a discussion of Apple products like iPhones, iPads, and Apple Watches. Why do people rush out to get the newest version every year and even camp out

32. Chi, "Three Types of Conceptual Change," 63. Scholars and practitioners of transformative learning likewise cite the effectiveness of metaphors and stories—especially great works of literature—for effecting dramatic changes in learners' meaning perspectives (Greene, "Realizing Literature's Emancipatory Potential").

over night to be among the first? What allure do these products hold? They promise to make us more powerful, more knowledgeable, more physically fit. After some discussion, the teacher can pivot upon the image of the apple into a discussion of the fruit Adam and Eve took from the forbidden tree. What was the allure of this fruit? How does the temptation distract or lead people away from God? As with Jesus' parables, this pivot from a familiar image to a more provocative one creates a rupture in learners' imagining and invites re-examination.

Such an experience of disorientation is a crucial moment of growth, particularly for critical meaning-makers. In their encounter with a mystifying Christian symbol, a peer's experience that is radically unlike their own, or the sheer complexity of today's world, learners are confronted with their inability to make sense of things within their current framework. Their foundations having been shaken, many begin to cast about for something more stable.

PROPOSING MORE ADEQUATE WAYS OF IMAGINING

We all seek meaning for our lives, but often we look for meaning in the wrong places—in professional status, in the opinions of others, in the possessions we acquire. Contemporary culture intensifies this struggle by marginalizing religion as a primary source of meaning and by presenting an endless parade of distractions and alternative visions of the good life. Part of the aim of Movement 2 of the SEE approach is to expose the inadequacy of these substitutes for deep meaning. Such was the focus of the first part of this chapter. However, many people today are already painfully aware of the dearth of meaning in their lives. Regardless of whether learners arrived in the classroom searching for deeper meaning for their lives or they have only just realized the limitations of their manner of meaning-making through exercises like those described above, the next step towards a conversion and rehabilitation of the imagination is giving them access to Christian symbols that evoke a vision of a fuller way of life.[33] This is the second aspect of what I mean by expanding the imagination.

---

33. Again, I am writing from the perspective of a Christian educator. However, religious educators from other religious traditions can surely think of classic symbols from their own traditions that invite learners to reimagine their lives.

Symbols that Enlighten and Heal

Following David Tracy, I have described the religious classic as a symbol, text, person, or event that not only disturbs us but also illuminates and integrates our experiences. Reading the Gospels, it is clear that Jesus' disciples experienced him as such a source of illumination. When Jesus asks the apostles if they also find his teaching too disturbing to continue following him, Peter responds, "Lord, to whom can we go? You have the words of eternal life" (John 6:68, NRSV). The author of the first letter of John echoes these sentiments:

> We declare to you . . . what we have heard, what we have seen with our eyes, what we have looked at and touched with our hands, concerning the word of life . . . and declare to you the eternal life that was with the Father and was revealed to us . . . so that you also may have fellowship with us . . . so that our joy may be complete. (1 John 1:1–4, NRSV)

These traces of the human encounter with the incarnate Son of God testify to how Jesus illuminated and invigorated the lives of his followers.

People have continued to find a light for their lives in Jesus all throughout history and into the present day. They experience this illumination in many ways—in private prayer, in the church's liturgy, in fellowship with other Christians, as well as in reflection on Jesus and the other Christian symbols they encounter in the sacraments, Scripture, theological texts, Christian art, and elsewhere. In the waters of baptism they recognize the reality of human sin, their need for forgiveness, and the possibility of receiving healing through the gift of God's love and mercy. In the church they see the possibility of community based not on politics, ideology, or ethnicity but rather on unconditional love and acceptance. These symbols reveal a different, fuller way of life. Those of us who have experienced these symbols and the inexhaustible meaning they bear can in retrospect recognize the superficiality and inadequacy of secular substitutes.

Still, as anyone who has tried to teach Shakespeare to high schoolers knows well, just because a text is a classic does not mean that learners will immediately respond to it or recognize its value. The teacher's skill and intentionality are indispensable for helping learners to engage the text with the kind of active imagination needed to immerse themselves in the deep waters of the text's meaning.

As I have worked to hone this skill over the years, I have learned that it pays to linger with these symbols and stories. Like ripening fruit or aging wine, classic Christian texts reward patience by yielding ever greater richness. This insight has given rise to two approaches to reading that have allowed Christians through the centuries to enter more deeply into revelatory texts. The first is the ancient practice of *lectio divina*.[34] Traditionally this contemplative approach to reading follows four steps:

1. *lectio*, reading a brief passage (usually from Scripture) aloud or to oneself,

2. *meditatio*, reflecting upon the meaning of the text,

3. *oratio*, speaking to God about what is emerging from this reading, and

4. *contemplatio*, resting silently in God's presence and listening for what God may have to say.

The second is an imaginative mode of reading Scripture that Ignatius of Loyola called "composition of place."[35] This technique involves readers imagining themselves in the scene described in a particular passage. For example, a class reading the Genesis account of creation might imagine smelling the salty ocean and feeling the spray of the waters as they pull back from the emerging dry ground, seeing plants and trees springing up from the soil, and hearing the various squawks and roars of the beasts coming into being. Regrettably, modern formal education often habituates students to reading rapidly and superficially on account of the sheer amount of material they are required to cover. These two approaches, by contrast, encourage slow, engaged reading that enables readers to enter into the world of the text and unlock its meanings just as they might grow in intimate understanding of a lover upon whom they lavish their time and attention.

Symbolic Thinking and Rational Analysis

Although my focus in this book is the imagination, I must nevertheless emphasize that rational analysis and doctrinal formulations also play an indispensable (albeit a derivative) role in the Christian's growth toward mature faith. Engagement on the level of the imagination is the necessary precondition for conversion of worldviews. It is therefore imperative to keep

34. Cf. Lichtmann, *Teacher's Way*.
35. See Martin, *Jesuit Guide to (Almost) Everything*, 145–55.

learners' (and teachers') imaginations active during this second phase of the SEE process. However, this is not to say that teachers should refrain entirely from lecture or using technical language. The key is to strike a balance in the use of symbolic and explanatory language. If teachers overexplain the symbols and inundate learners with definitions and qualifications, they stifle the learners' imaginations, sap them of their interest in the topic, and diminish the chances they will make meaningful connections with their personal experiences. On the other hand, if teachers limit their teaching to symbolic expressions with no recourse to explanatory language, they withhold the intellectual resources learners need to understand their experiences clearly and to judge accurately what is real and true and what is not. Where symbols generate the energy upon which faith lives, doctrines counter fantastical and idolatrous thinking by keeping the heart and mind trained upon the ineffable mystery of God. To engage the imagination to the exclusion of the intellect is to risk abandoning pre-critical meaning-makers to their naïve images of God, self, and world and confirming critical meaning-makers' suspicions regarding the anti-intellectuality of religion.

When exploring faith, therefore, there comes a time when rational analysis becomes indispensable. The timing and extent of this analysis will vary with the age and psychological readiness of the learners, but, generally speaking, in the SEE approach, that time aligns with Movement 2. This is the moment when I have found it most effective to draw upon academic theology and ecclesial documents.[36] Having already stimulated the vital core of learners' meaning-making and drawn them in with the promise of meaningful Christian symbols, I have disposed students to perceive technical terms, definitions, doctrinal formulations, and rational arguments, not as instruments of intellectual torture but rather as tools for exploration. In the hands of people who now desire to examine the meaning of Christian symbols, these tools serve the invaluable function of clarifying thinking, revealing nuances, and separating fantastical imaginings from reality.

Although rational analysis is essential, I have nonetheless found that I personally am not pedagogically effective when I lecture for extended periods of time, even following an imaginatively stimulating exercise. Fortunately, I have found other means of integrating analysis into my teaching. The "talk aloud," for example, is a common pedagogical technique that helps

---

36. *The Catechism of the Catholic Church* provides the primary touchstone for Catholic educators like myself. Religious educators from other traditions can identify analogous resources in their own traditions.

to balance imaginative engagement with intellectual refinement. Following this technique, the teacher reads aloud with students, periodically externalizing his or her thought process for interpreting the meaning of the text. This approach has the benefit of keeping learners' focus on the text while allowing the teacher to incorporate on the fly background information, doctrinal clarifications, theological insights, and interpretive guidelines.[37]

My lesson on the Incarnation offers an illustration of how I have struck this balance in my teaching. After presenting students with visual representations of Jesus' entering into the mess of human existence—his birth in a stable, his passion, the crucifixion—I draw the students' attention back to the refrain of Vance Joy's song, in which the artist sings about sharing the body and mess of another. I suggest that this would be a fitting theme song for Jesus, who took on a human body and all the pain, suffering, and conflict that comes with being human. I then allow some time for students to process with one another what this implies about how God responds to the problem of sin and the mess it has made of human affairs. Finally, I connect these images with the doctrine of the hypostatic union of Christ's two natures (defined at the Council of Chalcedon in 451 CE). I remind students of their earlier conclusion that what is most helpful is for another person to simply be present to us while we are suffering, and I point out that this is precisely what God did for humanity. This observation helps to explain why Jesus became fully human and how his becoming human helps us to entrust ourselves to him. However, I add, besides entering into the messiness of our lives, God does what no human being can do for us, namely, healing our brokenness. That is why it is significant that Jesus is not only fully human but also fully divine.

Symbols that Invite (and Bear) Exploration

The way students encounter Jesus in the SEE approach is for many—even those raised Christian—a new experience. Previously they might have viewed Jesus as a dusty relic of the past, like Julius Caesar or Abraham Lincoln, or as a quasi-fictional character. Either way, he has little to do with them and their lives. However, when they approach Jesus as a living person and a classic symbol, the effect is palpable. Recognizing Jesus as God's response to human suffering—the very suffering they experience in their own lives—intrigues

37. For example, the norms for interpreting Scripture specified in the *Catechism of the Catholic Church*, no. 109–19.

them. Where many students are overwhelmed by the messiness of life in the postmodern world, Jesus and other Christian symbols intimate to them new existential possibilities. They present more adequate images of God, self, other, and world than those around which learners had previously attempted to build their lives. They raise questions of existential import. For example, reflecting on Jesus' Incarnation, passion, death, and resurrection leads them to wonder: Might there be cause for hope in the midst of the messiness of life? Might healing really be possible for the world and for me? Perhaps there is another way to respond to suffering other than despair or self-distraction. Might we overcome by bringing love into the midst of suffering and entering into solidarity with those who suffer?

For pre-critical learners and Christians who have never reflected critically upon their faith, such an encounter with a classic symbol provides the impetus to undertake that critical reflection and go deeper in their faith. For critical meaning-makers who are dismissive of religion, this encounter provides a different kind of wakeup call. Encountering a Christian symbol that suggests possibilities for a fuller mode of existence and generates a sense of excitement can prompt feelings of loss and longing in a student like Serena who has rejected religious symbolism and therefore lives in a flattened reality. Particularly if she sees joy and a sense of meaningfulness in her teacher or peers, they become a question to her: What do they have or know that I don't?

Of course, she may simply dismiss their enthusiasm as naiveté. Conscious that learners may respond this way, it becomes important for teachers to give learners the opportunity to examine and interrogate the symbols presented to them so they cannot dismiss them so easily. In general, this critical impulse is a natural part of development beyond pre-critical meaning-making, and for that reason teachers should encourage it. We should also encourage learners to explore the classic symbols of the Christian faith for the reason that they reveal more meaning when we do so. These symbols have an inherent power to captivate our imaginations, but we need to probe, interpret, analyze, and interrogate them in order to appropriate their meaning for our own lives. Another aim of Movement 2 in the SEE approach is thus to provide learners with the opportunity to do just this—not only to enter imaginatively into the reality these symbols open up but also to verify that reality for themselves.

Again, students' own questions play a crucial role. New ideas and images become most firmly rooted within our worldviews when they answer questions that are important to us. One way of explaining why so much education (including religious education) makes no meaningful impression upon learners is that teachers provide answers to questions that the students (and perhaps the teachers themselves) have never asked. If learners find that the meanings contained within these symbols illuminate their experiences and help to answer their questions, they will become a meaningful part of their worldview.

Having the space to ask real questions is especially important for critical meaning-makers who have dismissed religious meaning as irrational. I find that my receptivity to serious questions is another respect in which my theology and religious education classes differ from those that many of my students have experienced previously.[38] Sometimes students are reluctant to ask hard questions because their teachers reprimanded them for doing so in the past. However, once students see that I reward them for asking difficult questions, the floodgates open up. They want to know why the Bible appears to contradict scientific accounts of cosmogenesis and evolution. They ask if Jesus really existed. They challenge the Catholic belief that Jesus is truly present in the Eucharist. Because I encourage students to ask these questions, I am able to assess the source of their difficulty in making sense of Christian beliefs (e.g., a naïve, pre-critical understanding of revelation or a reduction of reality to empirically verifiable phenomena). This in turn enables me to provide answers—or, better yet, lead them to their own answers—that take seriously critical methods of inquiry while also drawing out the enduring meaning of Christian symbols and teachings.

This can be nerve-wracking business because it requires me as the teacher to relinquish some control. A student might ask a question I cannot answer, but that is a risk I must take. I cannot answer the questions I do not allow students to ask, and, if they do not ask the questions that arise for them, the symbols of the Christian faith will remain irrelevant to them. Only when critical learners see that the symbols at the heart of the Christian faith can bear rigorous scrutiny, that they bear meaning that is not incompatible with but rather deeper than what we can know by empirical investigation, do they begin to consider seriously that they might have missed something. Only then does it seem plausible to them that they might yet find meaning for their lives in these symbols. Discerning what it

---

38. According to the Saint Mary's Press and CARA study of Catholic disaffiliation, many former Catholics express frustration at never having their questions heard or answered (McCarty and Vitek, *Going, Going, Gone*, 22).

would actually look like for them again to embrace a Christian worldview will be the work of Movement 3.

HABITS OF A NEW INTERIORITY CULTIVATED IN MOVEMENT 2

By engaging in the exercises associated with Movement 2 of the SEE approach, learners can develop habits that are characteristic of post-critical meaning-making and therefore more adequate to making Christian sense of life in the postmodern world.

The first of these is a set of habits of critical self-reflection. Many of us are woefully neglectful of our own inner lives. As pointed out in chapter 2, this neglect of the inner life is practically a defining trait of contemporary Western culture. With so many external distractions presented to my students, they are typically more adept at curating their social media profiles than they are tending to the workings of their inner thoughts, imaginings, desires, and feelings. Fortunately, I have found that simply directing my students' attention to the existence of their inner life can be revolutionary for them. Still, remaining attentive to the inner life and becoming adept at regulating it is far more laborious.

The exercises described in the early part of this chapter (e.g., examining their mental images, considering different perspectives, asking big questions) provide the space and guidance learners need to cultivate these habits of self-reflection. After watching something like Eli Pariser's TED Talk, which explains how Google's algorithms progressively narrow the content each person views, most of my students suddenly become much more reflective about the images they consume.[39] With practice, they become more consistently attentive to how popular media, advertising, and other people are influencing their worldview. They likewise grow in awareness of their own assumptions, biases, and blind spots and in their willingness to question these. Empowered by this heightened self-awareness, they are better able to nurture relationships, create an environment, and make decisions that contribute to the integration of their interior lives.

In order for these new habits to take root, learners must practice them outside of instructional time and of their own volition. To this end, I have sometimes recommended that my students take up the practice of

---

39. Pariser, "Beware Online 'Filter Bubbles.'"

the daily examen.[40] A pillar of Ignatian spirituality, the examen involves reviewing the day with an eye to where God was present, to where one loved well and where one failed to love, and to one's emotional reactions to these recollections. Praying the examen is a simple way for learners to begin to incorporate practices of self-reflection like those learned in class into their daily routine.

A second habit that learners cultivate through participating in the exercises of Movement 2 (and Movement 3) is that of drawing from the deep wells of the Christian tradition. The SEE approach promotes growth in this new habit of imagining by (1) giving learners access to classic, revelatory symbols, stories, and rituals from the Christian tradition and (2) training learners in different methods of imaginatively exploring them. Today we are awash in images. Some are salutary, but many are simply distracting. Some are outright harmful to the interior life. We need symbols that illuminate our experience and provide the core of an integrating worldview. For millennia, Christians have found such illumination and integration in Jesus Christ, the reign of God, and the constellation of symbols that orbit around these.

Still, people—critical meaning-makers especially—have to experience the power of these symbols in order to have a reason to give them a more central role in their imagining than the American flag or a political campaign slogan or the Apple logo. Such is the benefit of engaging learners in imaginative practices of theological reflection like *lectio divina* and composition of place and taking a similarly reflective, imaginative approach to viewing movies, icons, and artwork. Engaging the imaginative riches of the Christian tradition in these ways, many of my students have experienced Christianity as more relevant and meaningful than they ever had before. Saint Augustine is no longer a two-dimensional stained-glass figure; he becomes a role model for young people facing peer pressure and worldly enticements. The crucifix is no longer a mere wall adornment; it becomes a symbol of God's love and of hope for overcoming history's cycle of violence. Many critical meaning-makers in particular discover in these classic symbols more profound meaning than they could ever create for themselves. When the semester ends, many of my students depart with a stronger inclination to return to these stories, figures, and images when life

---

40. For a guide to the examen, see https://www.ignatianspirituality.com/ignatian -prayer/the-examen.

confronts them with big questions as well as a set of practices for exploring these symbols' inexhaustible meaning.

A third habit that learners develop by regularly participating in the exercises of Movement 2 is that of interpreting symbols, or as Ricoeur calls it, "thinking *from* symbols" as opposed to "living *in* symbols."[41] This habit benefits both pre-critical and critical meaning-makers. As Lonergan observes, pre-critical meaning-makers often mistakenly believe something to be real so long as it "is the object of a sufficiently integrated and a sufficiently intense flow of sensitive representations, feelings, words, and actions."[42] The result is a susceptibility to fantasy and idolatry that can cause them to lose touch with God and with reality. I see this susceptibility in some of my students, who unreflectively view the world through the engineered lens of social media. Critical meaning-makers, for their part, often reject religious symbols and symbolic knowing altogether and in so doing deprive themselves of a necessary source of psychological integration and of connection with God. However, as Ricoeur argues, the onset of critical consciousness need not mean the irretrievable loss of religious symbols' meaning:

> But if we can no longer live the great symbolisms of the sacred in accordance with the original belief in them, we can, we modern men, aim at a second naïveté in and through criticism. In short, it is by *interpreting* that we can *hear* again. Thus it is in hermeneutics that the symbol's gift of meaning and the endeavor to understand by deciphering are knotted together.[43]

By engaging my students in the interpretive and questioning exercises of Movement 2, I strive to impress upon them the necessity of both critical inquiry and imaginative engagement for constructing meaning substantial enough to sustain a life worth living. Students learn how to accomplish this union of the analytical and imaginative in our weekly exploration of classic Christian texts, and gradually many will extend this approach to their own reading of Scripture, their participation in worship, and to prayer. Cultivating this more balanced approach to meaning-construction involves, on the one hand, becoming practiced in applying interpretive guidelines, refining their symbolic thinking with theory and doctrine, and asking critical questions about how they and others understand Christian symbols. At the same time, it involves a willingness to enter into the worldview generated

41. Ricoeur, "Hermeneutics of Symbols and Philosophical Reflection," 201.

42. Lonergan, *Insight*, 561.

43. Ricoeur, *Symbolism of Evil*, 351.

by these symbols in spite of—or rather through—their application of critical methods. In this way learners achieve in their imagining and meaning-making a union of critical reasoning with the fullness of meaning they previously enjoyed in their pre-critical phase.

Developing these habits (which I have associated with a "new interiority") takes time and practice. Usually it is only towards the end of the semester that I see them beginning to take hold. Such development also typically requires a disruption or series of disruptions in order to loosen the hold of unhealthy or maladaptive habits. For pre-critical Christians, this disruption involves bursting the bubble of their naïve imaginings in order to kickstart more critical, self-aware meaning-making. For many critical meaning-makers, it takes a powerful encounter with a classic Christian symbol (or person) to overcome their skepticism of religion and help them to seek meaning once again in something beyond their own powers of reason.

CONCLUSION

Terms like "disruption" and "conversion" are likely to make some readers uncomfortable. Today's educators are wary of anything that smacks of coercion or manipulation, and rightly so. To be clear, the intent of this approach is not to coerce learners of different faiths into converting to Christianity. Students may decide to change religious affiliations on account of their learning experience, but that is not my aim. The purpose of SEE is, rather, to invite learners to undergo a conversion in their imagining to Jesus' vision of the reign of God. It is an invitation in the sense that I strive to help them catch a glimpse of how Jesus' vision can give meaning and coherence to their lives. If they are intrigued (and many are), I offer them guidance in exploring this vision further. If not, I do not compel them to do so by means of how I grade them, how I treat them in class, or in any other way. How I employ this approach depends on the context. If I am teaching a parish Confirmation class, I am free to be more explicit about the life of discipleship to which the students are committing themselves by receiving this sacrament. If I am teaching a class of first-year college students that includes non-Christians, I present our engagement with Christian symbols as an opportunity for students to examine their meaning-making more generally.[44]

---

44. Although I have never taught at a secular institution, I imagine that many aspects of the SEE approach could be adapted for that context just as contemplative teaching practices (e.g., *lectio divina*) have been adapted for use in secular institutions.

All these qualifications aside, SEE does invite conversion, and conversion is an inherently discomforting experience. It involves disruption of our accustomed ways of constructing meaning and our illusions of self-sufficiency. This experience can leave us feeling disarmed and disoriented. Although learners typically need to undergo a significant disruption on their way to developing a more adequate form of meaning-making, it would be negligence of the highest order for teachers to abandon their students in their disoriented state. As Robert Kegan explains, "People grow best when they continuously experience an ingenious blend of support and challenge," of "continuity" as well as "contradiction."[45] Movement 2 of SEE provides some degree of support and continuity insofar as learners' encounter with the illuminating, integrating power of classic Christian symbols and their training in post-critical habits of imagining show them a way forward to a fuller, more meaningful life. However, this concern to support learners through their tumultuous transition moves front and center in Movement 3, as we are about to see.

However, for now I leave it to educators working in such contexts to imagine what would be appropriate.

45. Kegan, *In Over Our Heads*, 42.

chapter 6

MOVEMENT 3: EMBRACING A NEW WAY OF IMAGINING

"Having robbed us of the certainties of our given world, [Jesus' parables] would leave us at the brink of relativity, naked and totally vulnerable before the divine mystery that is God."[1] In the previous chapter, we saw how, like Jesus' parables, Movement 2 of the SEE approach brings to light the faultiness of learners' self-assurances and self-reliance in order to open them up to receiving and co-creating a fuller, more adequate worldview. While such disruption is often necessary, it is never an end in itself. Jesus undoubtedly confounded his audiences, but, as we will see later in the chapter, he did not leave them to flounder. Neither should we religious educators abandon our students to confusion, whether it be confusion arising within the learning process or from their everyday experiences of life in an increasingly complex world.

THE GOAL OF MOVEMENT 3

The sad reality is that many of today's young people do feel lost and forsaken.[2] They feel that the church and other institutions have failed them.[3] More generally, growing up in postmodern culture with all its complexities and contradictions has left them feeling that they lack a clear sense of direction in life.[4] Some readers will wonder how today's young people could

1. Conn, *Christian Conversion*, 214.
2. McCarty and Vitek, *Going, Going, Gone*, 18.
3. Pew Research Center, "Millennials in Adulthood."
4. Smith, *Souls in Transition*, 292.

possibly feel lost. *Isn't this the generation that has been constantly coddled and directed by overly-involved parents?* The fact of the matter is that preparing young people for life in the postmodern world is no easy task. Even parents and teachers with the best of intentions can fail to provide their children and students with what they truly need.

Experts like Robert Kegan explain that promoting learners' development requires just the right balance of challenge and support.[5] Neglecting either one can leave learners ill-prepared to meet the mental demands of postmodern life. On the one hand, while educators who insist on more "rigorous" catechesis (i.e., heavier on doctrine) likely have the best of intentions, they can become so fixated on instilling a solid understanding of doctrine that they fail to prepare learners to live out their faith in today's world. Parents of millennials have come under fire for doing too much for their children—planning their schedules, solving their problems, even writing their papers—with the result that their children enter adulthood unprepared to deal with the realities of daily life. Religious education that is too narrowly focused on content runs a similar risk of sending future generations of Christians out into the postmodern world bearing Christian teachings wrapped up like mother-made lunches but unable to make meaning for themselves of either these teachings or the world in which they live. In other words, such an approach provides support but not the kind of challenge learners need to grow into mature meaning-makers.

On the other hand, challenging learners without providing adequate support is equally problematic. Such can sometimes be the case with more experiential approaches to faith formation such as school- and church-sponsored service projects. The first high school I taught in mandated that students complete a certain number of service hours as a requirement for graduation, but made no effort to facilitate the reflection needed for students to synthesize their experiences of service with their Christian beliefs and to appropriate its meaning for themselves.[6] In my conversations with Catholic educators around the country, I have frequently heard the same criticism of service programs in their schools and parishes. When students have been fortunate to engage in meaningful service in Appalachia or at the local soup kitchen, they often return talking excitedly about what an

---

5. Cf. Kegan, *In Over Heads*, 42.

6. Genuine service-learning programs that integrate service with carefully paired readings and class or group discussion offer a better model. See, e.g., Eyler et al., *Where's the Learning in Service-Learning*.

amazing experience it was and how they received more than they gave. However, too often, after a few months' time, their lives are in no way different than they were before. They did the service. What was missing was the support they needed to make sense of it.

In sum, preparing learners to live a life of Christian discipleship in postmodern society requires providing them with the right blend of challenge to grow beyond their limited ways of constructing meaning and support in appropriating new meanings when old ones have broken down. For many teachers, these demands necessitate that they adopt a new approach to religious education. I am offering the SEE process as one such approach. As concerns the need for challenge, the previous chapter discussed how engagement with Jesus' vision of the reign of God in Movement 2 of SEE challenges learners' limited ways of constructing meaning. In that chapter, I also began describing how SEE provides support to learners in Movement 2 by giving them access to revealed symbols that illuminate and integrate their experiences. However, supporting learners in their work of reintegration—what Kegan calls providing "continuity"—is the explicit aim of Movement 3.[7] In this chapter, I will explain how Movement 3 supports learners in embracing a more adequate way of imagining in two crucial ways: (1) by helping them to synthesize a new vision for their lives and (2) by inviting them to make the decision to pursue that vision. In this way, Movement 3 and the SEE approach as a whole help learners to recover the sense of integration and meaningfulness that is essential to the fullness of life Jesus promises.

GENERAL SUPPORTS FOR THE TRANSITION

Before getting into the specifics of how to help learners synthesize a new vision for life, it will be helpful to say something more generally about how to support learners through a period of disorientation. The transition from Movement 2 to Movement 3 is a delicate moment. Transformative learning theorist Jennifer Garvey Berger explains, when learners have had the foundations of their sense of reality shaken, "the past seems untenable and the future unidentifiable."[8] Because this sort of situation is extremely uncomfortable for us, we tend to grasp for any source of security close at hand. If learners are not to fall back into self-enclosed mentalities like

7. Kegan, *Evolving Self*, 258.
8. Garvey Berger, "Dancing on the Threshold," 344.

fundamentalism, tribalism, or nihilism, teachers need to provide learners with the assurance they require to abandon their sinking ship and push out into uncharted waters.

Teachers can provide this support in numerous ways, three of which I will highlight here. First, researchers from a variety of learning-related fields are consistent in emphasizing the importance of acknowledging and validating learners' feelings of confusion and anxiety.[9] Learners who are seeing their religion through a critical lens for the first time may feel betrayed by their religious community and experience a loss of their sense of identity. In the case of learners who had already abandoned a naïve form of faith at some earlier point, the experience of yet another loss—this time a loss of confidence in their own rational capacities—may leave them feeling that there simply is no ground for certainty in this life. In both cases, it may feel to learners like the world is ending. At such a moment, it helps to know that this feeling will not last forever. In this regard, Mezirow highlights the benefit of learners receiving the assurance that others have shared the discontent that they are currently experiencing and eventually overcame it. Kegan similarly points out the value of helping learners recognize that they have successfully made their way through such transformations in the past.[10]

Implicit in this advice regarding validating learners' feelings is an insight into the importance of relationships in the learning process. The support of a community is the second crucial element for weathering dramatic change of any sort. In this regard, experiencing a major loss of meaning in our life is akin to losing a loved one. The world seems to be ending. We cannot make sense of things. It is hard to imagine how we will go on. As my students have observed, what we yearn for most deeply in such times of loss is not an explanation for our suffering (although we seek that too) but rather the compassionate presence of someone who cares. Jesus did not always offer clear explanations or straight answers to people's questions. What he does more consistently is initiate relationships and invite people to be with him.[11] My appreciation for this relational dimension of Jesus' teaching has grown as time and again I see learners in transition finding reassurance in the accompaniment of an empathetic teacher, mentor, or peer. Often these

9. Taylor, "Analyzing Research on Transformative Learning Theory," 303; Kegan, "What 'Form' Transforms?," 35–70; Haughton, *Transformation of Man*, 38; Coffman, "Inclusive Language as a Means of Resisting Hegemony"; Morgan, "Displaced Homemaker Programs"; Sveinunggaard, "Transformative Learning in Adulthood."

10. See Kegan, "What 'Form' Transforms?," 58–59.

11. See, for example, John 1:38–39.

supporting figures serve as a guide and model for how the learner can move forward. Even when they cannot give learners the answers they seek, there seems to be comfort in wrestling with the questions together.

Jesus' example suggests a third insight into how to support people when their world has been overturned, namely, by using humor. Humor has the power to give perspective and to help us see things in a more positive light. It has a way of loosening us up and alleviating the mental tension created by the disruption of our accustomed meanings. It mitigates the sense of perceived threat on the emotional level because we associate humor primarily with positive feelings and benign intentions. By adding an element of humor to his parables, Jesus was able to challenge his audience while softening the resistance and resentment that his stories might (and often did) elicit.[12]

Jesus' humor often took the form of exaggeration and hyperbole. For example, he tells a story of a servant who owes 10,000 talents, which in modern terms would be like saying he owed several billion dollars. No single person—no matter how prodigal—could possibly amass such a debt. The mere thought of it is laughable. In another parable, a woman hides some yeast in three measures of flour (somewhere between 40 and 60 pounds), a similarly outlandish amount. Many times I have witnessed the benefits of humor in my classroom. A well-timed self-effacing joke or a playful nudge at a student can provide a much needed psychological release when things are getting tense and help learners to relax their mental clenching enough to allow new ways of thinking to emerge.

SYNTHESIZING A NEW VISION

In Movement 2 (or perhaps before they even arrived in class), learners have experienced a breakdown of familiar yet limited forms of meaning-making. On the positive side, breakdowns are the necessary prelude to the differentiations of consciousness that attend normal human development and usher in new cognitive abilities. Still, a differentiation of consciousness is fundamentally a disruption of a former state of psychological equilibrium or integration. The price paid for advance into critical consciousness is the loss of the fullness of meaning enjoyed within a pre-critical worldview. This loss of integration is uncomfortable, and the signs of this discomfort in contemporary US society—a precipitous rise

---

12. Cf. Levine, *Short Stories by Jesus*, 276.

in mental health issues, increases in drug and alcohol abuse, rising sui-
cide rates—are now impossible to ignore.

As more and more people internalize the critical consciousness emanating from modernity, the urgency of addressing this lack of integration
grows. In order to recover a life that is more whole, such people will have
to undergo a further reintegration of consciousness that incorporates the
critical capacities and meanings gained through the critical differentiation
into a more integral, more stable synthesis. All three movements of the SEE
process play an important role in facilitating learners' reintegration, but it is
in Movement 3 that the cumulative effect becomes most evident.

Tapping into the Integrating Power of Symbols

One of the first major steps in my journey toward what eventually became
the SEE approach was coming to recognize the unique power of symbols.
Over the years, I noticed that the more I focused our learning time on stories
and symbols, the more my students seemed to come alive in class. When
I began researching the role of images and symbols in human cognition, I
discovered that their power extends far beyond capturing learners' attention.
Symbols possess an inherent power to facilitate our psychological and existential integration, and they do so in numerous ways. Concerning symbols'
role in facilitating internal communication, Lonergan observes:

> Organic and psychic vitality have to reveal themselves to inten-
> tional consciousness and, inversely, intentional consciousness has
> to secure the collaboration of organism and psyche. Again, our
> apprehensions of values occur in intentional responses, in feelings:
> here too it is necessary for feelings to reveal their objects and, in-
> versely, for objects to awaken feelings. It is through symbols that
> mind and body, mind and heart, heart and body communicate.[13]

Besides facilitating internal communication, symbols promote a sense
of wholeness in our lives in other ways. As images that are partly concrete
and yet intellectually inexhaustible, they enable us to imagine, name, ask
about, and grow in understanding of what is initially unknown (e.g., God,
the world, ourselves, and the other) and to achieve some level of internal
integration in the absence of complete knowledge.[14] Since we never acquire

---

13. Lonergan, *Method in Theology*, 66–67; cf. Langer, *Philosophy in a New Key*, 289.

14. Lonergan, *Insight*, 557.

complete knowledge in this life, serve a crucial purpose throughout our lives. However, they prove particularly valuable in times of existential disorientation insofar as they give us something to hold onto when conceptually bound meanings fail.

Again, Jesus' parables offer an illustrative example. In the previous chapter, I noted how Jesus sometimes pivots upon a familiar image into a discomforting vision. However, in the parables these "pivot" images serve not only to disrupt but also to support his hearers cognitively as they transition into a new experience of reality. They allow the hearers to keep one foot planted in the familiar while stepping with the other into an unfamiliar and uncomfortable world of meaning.[15] Even as images like the mustard seed or yeast confound the audience's usual ways of thinking about God's reign, the familiarity of the image itself provides some limited sense of continuity. The image sticks in their minds and provides a jumping off point in their search for a new understanding of God's reign.

Although an ambiguous image might not seem like much to seize upon, we should not overlook the value of such seeds of meaning. Existing in a meaning vacuum is intolerable for human beings. Some people end their own lives rather than endure this situation. In this regard, the words of Scripture ring true: "Where there is no vision, the people perish" (Prov 29:18, KJV). While the loss of the vision that guides our lives is devastating—even fatal—we can survive the lesser disruption of particular beliefs and conceptual understandings so long as we have something else to which to cling. This is a crucially important insight for today's religious educators. Symbols provide the life raft learners need to stay afloat when the arcs of meaning that carry them through life have been swamped by the storms of postmodern culture.

Robert Kegan's research confirms the value of symbolic expression in the midst of developmental transitions. He suggests that images and metaphorical language are particularly well suited to helping learners establish new meanings, especially when employed with an ear to learners' own usage. Kegan explains, "A metaphor is interpretive, but it is an interpretation made in soft clay rather than cold analysis. It invites the client to put his hands on it and reshape it into something more fitting to him."[16] The malle-

---

15. Kegan's concept of an "evolutionary bridge" holds a similar meaning of a support or context for crossing over from an old understanding of self to a new self (Kegan, *In Over Our Heads*, 43).

16. Kegan, *In Over Our Heads*, 260.

ability of symbols and metaphors provides learners with a mental space or "holding environment" for generating and experimenting with new meanings when old meanings have disintegrated.[17]

Of course, not all symbols are created equal in this regard. The image of the successful business executive that motivated a woman through her schooling and early career may deflate when, after working tirelessly for years and achieving the position she desired, she realizes that her work is not meaningful to her. A man who has constructed an identity for himself partly around always having the newest technology may discover how shallow the meaning of his favorite tech brands runs when he is laid off and can no longer afford yearly upgrades.

Classic Christian symbols, by contrast, bear a deeper meaning capable of sustaining a fully human life, particularly when we are struggling to find meaning elsewhere.[18] As mentioned earlier, many of my students readily identify with the experience of life as a big mess. Many, at least from time to time, struggle to make sense of it all. In my lesson on the Incarnation, I do not attempt to explain away the messiness of life. It simply is not possible to do so—certainly not in a 75-minute class period. Yet, despite lacking a clear account of reality that dispels life's confusion, my students find mental and emotional support in the image of Jesus on the cross, the symbol of God's presence with us amidst our suffering. This image and other classic symbols that students encounter in our course (e.g., the promised land of Exodus, Dante's pilgrimage toward the beatific vision, the Eucharist that fueled Dorothy Day's service to the poor) do not explain away the mysteries and paradoxes of life, but they do provide reference points for students' ongoing search for meaning.

Judging the Adequacy of Symbols and Interpretations

Although learners can find a life raft in classic symbols when accustomed meanings have been swept away, in the words of Thich Nhat Hahn, "the raft is not the shore."[19] They cannot cling to a life raft forever. Living life to

---

17. Kegan, *Evolving Self*, 116.

18. As mentioned in the previous chapter, other religious traditions have their own classics. Although I will speak primarily of Christian symbols in this chapter, I encourage those from other religious backgrounds to read on with the classic symbols from their own traditions in mind.

19. Nhat Hahn and Berrigan, *Raft Is Not the Shore*.

the fullest means living from a sense of meaning and purpose, not merely surviving. Achieving this kind of stability and direction requires that learners do more than toy with the symbols of the Christian tradition. It requires making personal judgments on the value and meaningfulness of these symbols. When they render their own well-founded judgments, the meanings offered to them become something even better than life rafts or distant lighthouses that give them hope of reaching safe harbor. They become solid rock upon which they can begin to build a new house of meaning in which to live. Encouraging learners to make their own reasoned judgments thus becomes a crucial task for religious educators in the work of helping them to synthesize a new vision for their lives.

On a basic psychological level, rendering judgment upon the truth or value of the content others convey to us makes it more meaningful to us. Although symbols bear an excess of meaning, they do not magically infuse that meaning into our lives, nor do we receive meaning from symbols simply because someone tells us they are meaningful. If Christian symbols are to play a meaningful role in learners' reconstruction of their worldview, they need to make their own judgments about the meaningfulness of the cross or the Eucharist, as they do for the political or brand stickers they put on their laptops or the pins they attach to their backpacks to express support for a social cause.

Some teachers might chafe at the suggestion to give learners the option to disregard Christian teaching, but the reality is that learners will render their own judgments upon these symbols one way or another. Many today are expressing a judgment on teachings they perceive as irrelevant or empty by walking away from the church. Explicitly inviting learners to make a judgment in the classroom where the teacher can respond to questions and objections improves the likelihood that learners will recognize the meaningfulness of these symbols for themselves. Several exercises of Movement 3, which I describe below, serve precisely this purpose.

Beyond their role in appropriating meaning, acts of judgment constitute the most crucial function in the cognitive process by which we ascertain truth.[20] To experience a symbol or life in general as meaningful is not a guarantee that our interpretations or living are in accord with the truth of the way things really are. People in a pre-critical culture may find an abundance of meaning in their religious symbols and rituals, but those

---

20. Here I presume the account of knowing and objectivity that Lonergan expounds in his *Insight*.

symbols and rituals may be full of superstition. Likewise, an adolescent boy's immersion in the world of a video game like *Grand Theft Auto* may imbue his days with energy and vividness. He may even experience a sense of integration in his living to the extent that he replicates in real life the reprehensible actions that further his aims in the game. However, this sense of vividness and integration derives from the intensity of the images in that video game, not their adequacy to representing reality as it is. Although this boy's imagination is highly stimulated, he is not exercising his capacity for judgment sufficiently to ground his active imagination.

The ability to make personal judgments of truth and value is particularly important in cultures like that of the contemporary United States. When the available information and meanings were relatively few and stable (as in the pre-modern and even the modern era), it was easier for a given community to evaluate, form a consensus about, and correct deviant meanings. In the current postmodern context, by contrast, fabricated images and misleading information are too abundant and generated too quickly for any given community to keep up. While communal checks on meaning remain important, this state of affairs makes it more necessary for individuals to develop the capacity to judge the veracity and value of the diverse meanings they encounter.

In this regard, the capacity for critical meaning-making (including critical judgment) is a practical necessity for people living in postmodern societies and therefore a capacity religious educators should cultivate in learners. We can nurture this capacity by asking questions that raise learners' awareness of the meanings carried in the images presented to them, whether in a religious education classroom or in their local mall. Such questions might include:

- Who crafted these images (e.g., inspired authors or a corporate marketing team)?

- What are their motivations for showing me these images (e.g., drawing me into relationship with God or getting me to buy a product)?

- What values and potential biases underlie these images (e.g., self-giving love or consumerism)?

- Are these consistent with my values and those of the Christian tradition? How do they make me feel? How do they affect my behavior?

In my own practice, I have found Movement 1 (after engaging personal experiences and images) and Movement 3 (after engaging Christian symbols) to be the most natural places to pose such questions. Repeating questioning exercises like these week after week, learners develop an open yet critical attitude to the images presented to them not only by their pastors and catechists but also on social media, Netflix, and Google ads. They cultivate a habit of asking questions about the images foisted upon them and about their own imagining rather than passively absorbing whatever images their environment presents to them.

Although the capacity for critical judgment is crucially important, we can overemphasize it to our own detriment. Critical meaning-makers recognize and seek to correct the characteristic error of pre-critical meaning-makers, the failure to judge their imaginings by reasonable criteria. This impulse becomes problematic for critical meaning-makers when they apply criteria that are so narrow (namely, the standards of rational argumentation and empirical verification) that they marginalize symbolic, tacit modes of thought in their meaning-making.

As we have seen, the rejection of symbol and ritual leads to psychological dis-integration and a perceived lack of meaning in life. In today's world, living a life that is not only grounded in reality but also integrated and authentically Christian requires of Christians a manner of constructing meaning that involves neither naïve immersion in religious symbols nor scrutinizing reality through an excessively rationalistic lens but rather deliberately judging the adequacy of their interpretations of those symbols. In a word, it requires a post-critical form of meaning-making characterized by the union of symbolic thinking and critical judgment.

Here, too, my teaching has been influenced by Jesus' example. Jesus' parables typically bear the character of an argument that entices us to make a judgment upon the situations and characters he describes. In making these judgments, we are almost always making an indirect judgment upon ourselves. Such is the case in the parable of the good Samaritan wherein Jesus invites the lawyer to render a judgment upon the characters of the parable and then reflects the lawyer's judgment back upon himself: "Go and do likewise" (Luke 10:37, NRSV). Thus drawing the lawyer into the drama of the parable, Jesus forces him to consider whether he himself has been a good neighbor to others. Inspired by Jesus' model, it has become my habit of ending every learning event by posing questions that invite learners to judge for themselves the topics we have been discussing. I ask them to consider:

- Do these Christian symbols help me to make sense of my experiences?

- Do they stimulate my thinking?

- Do I sense something significant in these symbols?

One thing that becomes abundantly clear in Jesus' teaching—in his parables particularly—is that God's ways are not our ways and that Jesus' standards of judgment are not those of the world.[21] Sin and bias can distort our values and motivations. Furthermore, as we have just been discussing, the influence of modern culture can contribute to reductionistic criteria for what counts as good and true, failing to take into account human needs and the limits of human knowing. Influenced as we are by modern critical methodology, our capacity to make sound judgments concerning the value of images hinges upon expanding our understanding of what constitutes appropriate criteria for judgment.

Above and beyond the basic question of whether a given symbol embodies something true of reality (an important criteria in itself), more adequate judgments will take into account existential and theological criteria. On the existential side, we ought to judge the value of symbols by their capacity for illumination and integration, that is, by how well they help us make sense of and give coherence to our experiences.[22] For example, when students find themselves resonating with the image of a crucified God, they are able to discover some meaning in their suffering, which alleviates the feeling that their world is falling apart. This existential resonance is an indication that this symbol merits further exploration.

Thomas Groome, synthesizing Scripture and authoritative theological voices, suggests "continuity," "community," and "consequences" as three theological criteria for judging the authenticity of a symbol or its interpretation.[23] First, we ought to judge symbols according to their continuity with the core truths and values of Christianity, especially Jesus' teachings about

21. See, for example, Matt 12:1–8; Mark 8:33; Luke 21:1–4.

22. Tracy, *Analogical Imagination*, 108.

23. Groome, *Sharing Faith*, 235. In many respects the judging activities of Movement 3 of the SEE approach align with those Groome prescribes for Movement 4 of his shared praxis approach. Likewise, the exercises aimed at inviting decision that I describe in the following section align with the activities of Movement 5 of shared praxis.

the reign of God.[24] Second, we should strongly favor union with the beliefs held in common by the Christian community as constituted by the official magisterium, the research of theological experts, and the *sensus fidelium*.[25] Finally, we must judge symbols as we do those who claim to be Christian, namely, "by their fruits" (Matt 7:20, NRSV), which is to say by the extent to which they engender love of God and neighbor.[26]

Because different criteria are often operating in the background of learners' minds, it is beneficial to discuss the above criteria explicitly with them. However, as is the case with any kind of meaningful learning, it is not sufficient to provide these criteria to learners on a handout or to force students to memorize them. I have learned that, if these existential and theological criteria are to become an ingrained, habitual part of learners' judging, they need to practice utilizing them.

It has thus become my habit in the SEE approach to imbed these existential and theological criteria in questions that I pose to learners repeatedly (in different formulations) as we engage different texts and symbols each week. For example, at the end of my Incarnation lesson, I ask my students to imagine what it would look like for them to respond to the messes of life in a way similar to Jesus and then to reflect in writing on how helpful they find Jesus' example of how to respond to the messiness of life. I invite my students to make a similar judgment when we have finished reading Dorothy Day's *The Long Loneliness*. This book includes the author's reflections on her experiences of loneliness as well as stories about the Catholic Worker and the community she helped to build there, a community of people loving and serving one another, putting others before themselves, and striving to live their lives as God wishes. I invite students to imagine what their lives would look like if they were part of this kind of community and to judge whether such loving community might in fact be the answer to our loneliness, as Day suggests.

Beyond simply asking questions that elicit learners' judgments, Groome suggests inviting learners to express their judgments through speaking, writing, drawing, aesthetic expression, journaling, movement, role playing, panel discussions, debates, and other activities.[27] As Groome's

---

24. Groome, *Sharing Faith*, 236; cf. Newman, *Essay on the Development of Doctrine*, 178–80.

25. Groome, *Sharing Faith*, 237.

26. Groome, *Sharing Faith*, 236.

27. Groome, *Sharing Faith*, 258.

list of activities suggests, sometimes learners need to feel their way into a judgment or creatively explore the possibilities suggested by the Christian symbols before making a judgment. In addition to the activities Groome describes, such exploration can take the form of learners telling stories or sketching out what a personal symbol system consistent with that of Christianity would look like for them.

As learners consistently recognize the illuminating and integrating power of Christian symbols and the benefits of aligning themselves with a two thousand-year old wisdom tradition, their criteria for what is good and true expands to become more commensurate with the fullness of reality and the fully human life God desires for us.

Shaping a Personal Vision

When we render a personal judgment upon the truth and value of a symbol, it ceases to be something hypothetical or external to us. In judging we make it our own. Acts of judgment are thus an essential component in constructing—or, more accurately, co-constructing—a personal worldview and vision for life. To use the language of "co-constructing" is to indicate that developing a worldview is not only a matter of affirming what is given to us. We make our own contributions insofar as we invite the Christian symbols we inherit into an ongoing dance with the images and understandings that emerge from our lived experiences. To this end, once learners have judged the adequacy of Christian symbols and of their own imagining, teachers should encourage them to address the question that inevitably arises next: What would a Christian way of life look like for me personally? Even though this question naturally presents itself when we judge that something is true and worthwhile, it is important that teachers make the question explicit for learners lest they put it off or ignore it.

I have already discussed how my Incarnation lesson offers one example of how to raise this question. To offer another example, at the end of a learning event centered around the creation stories of Genesis 1–2, the teacher might ask learners to decide how concretely they could show respect for themselves and others who are likewise created in the image of God. For a learning event about Jesus' parable of the good Samaritan, learners might envision how to be better neighbors to the people they encounter in their lives. Responses may be written or not, but regardless teachers best serve learners by allowing adequate time for them to reflect seriously on the question and to visualize the action in vivid detail.

These examples illustrate how teachers might help learners to live out particular aspects of the Christian life. However, the reader will recall that the more ambitious aim of SEE, more than merely appropriating particular aspects of Christianity, is helping learners synthesize a coherent, life-giving worldview in cooperation with God's gift of meaning. With this end in mind, teachers should also provide learners with opportunities to envision their lives as a whole through the lens of Jesus' vision of the reign of God. Such opportunities might include inviting learners to write out or share with one another their life story as they have come to see it in light of the common human story of creation, sin, and redemption. Alternatively, learners might give expression to their new worldview through artistic projects like painting, sculpting, or musical composition. Again, because it takes time for a new worldview to coalesce, these activities will be most fruitful when teachers are generous in the time they allocate to them.

The more vivid learners' vision is, the more likely they are to act upon it. In the words of Lonergan, knowledge "can become effective in [our] concrete living only if the content . . . can be embodied in images that release feeling and emotion and flow spontaneously into deeds no less than words."[28] Evidence for the efficaciousness of visualization exercises abounds in the testimonies of star athletes and musicians as well as in neuroscientific research.[29] This evidence corroborates the basic pattern of human thinking I described in chapter 1: Mental images derived from concrete experience provide the basis for thought. We refine our thinking by means of abstract reasoning, concepts, and judgments. Before thought translates into action, it once again returns from abstraction to the concreteness of images.

MAKING THE DECISION TO LIVE INTO GOD'S REIGN

In the preceding pages, I have been discussing the pedagogical strategies I and others have found helpful as learners work to synthesize a new vision for their lives: Learners imaginatively engage Christian symbols with the power to give meaning and coherence to their experiences. They judge the value and meaningfulness of these symbols for themselves. Finally, they

---

28. Lonergan, *Insight*, 570.
29. Barbezat and Bush, *Contemplative Practices in Higher Education*, 25–26.

weave the meanings these symbols evoke together with the images and experiences arising within their own lives.

Guiding learners through these activities, the SEE process provides them with the support and challenge they need to achieve what so many are lacking today, namely, a coherent worldview that gives meaning and wholeness to their lives. As we have seen in the foregoing chapters, forging such a vision for life in the postmodern context involves overcoming significant obstacles. Now, having constructed (or reconstructed) this vision, learners come to confront yet another challenge and a crucial moment of decision: Will they pursue this vision or not? Throughout the course of a semester, many of my students' imaginative capabilities grow increasingly adaptive and more authentically Christian. However, I try to help my students to recognize that knowing is not yet doing. If their desire is for Jesus' vision to take hold of their lives in a definitive way, they must make a personal decision to live into that vision.

To put it another way, decision is the final necessary step in consummating the process of conversion towards which the whole SEE process has been building. The reader will recall that decision is a key element that distinguishes conversion from natural psychological development. From a psychological perspective, learners arrive at this decision-point when a less adequate form of meaning-making has broken down and the possibility of another has come into focus. Pedagogically speaking, a teacher can lead learners to this point by making the limitations of the old form more apparent, proposing more adequate alternatives, and providing support as learners reconstruct their meaning framework. Theologically speaking, it is up to God to give learners the grace to overcome the fears, biases, egoism and moral impotence preventing them from entering into a new way of life. Once the learner arrives at this moment, however, the decision is theirs and theirs alone.

Jesus' example suggests possibilities for how teachers can encourage learners to make a decision to live into an authentically Christian vision of life. His parables in particular have a way of eliciting a personal response. For example, at the end of the parable of the good Samaritan, Jesus asks the lawyer who was neighbor to the victim. The lawyer answers, "The one who showed him mercy," and Jesus responds, "Go and do likewise" (Luke 10:37, NRSV). In this way, Jesus turns the lawyer's judgment back upon himself, and now he must confront the decision of whether he will enact the vision of compassion Jesus has set before his eyes. The parable's inviting familiarity, coupled with its open-endedness, encourages this man to blend his life story with the narrative of the parable and to see himself in its characters. For our part, if we engage Jesus' parables seriously, we too will find it hard to remain indifferent to them, for we recognize our lives at stake therein. Once we enter into Jesus' vision of the reign of God, we cannot in good conscience continue living as before. Following such a conversion of the imagination, we must choose either to undergo a conversion in our living or to live at odds with ourselves.

In my experience, providing learners with opportunities for meaningful decisions utterly transforms the learning experience. Doing so brings Christian teachings down from the ethereal realm of ideas into the concrete world of everyday life. Suddenly things get real. It is not necessary to put learners on the spot by demanding that they announce their decision to the classroom. In other settings (e.g., on retreats, in sacramental preparation, in the context of worship), doing so may have the effect of providing others with an inspiring witness. However, when teaching university courses or in parish religious education programs, it is perfectly effective to prompt learners to make a decision privately. Most commonly, I invite learners to commit mentally or to write down for themselves how they will live out their new vision. As the teacher, I do not need to know what they decide. They know, and God knows.

Learners are more likely to persist in their decisions if they have opportunities to express them concretely. Obviously there are constraints on what teachers are able to do within the classroom context or by means of occasional excursions, but teachers can engage learners in classroom activities that help to bridge decision and action. Most basically, learners can develop a plan of action specifying how they will act upon their decisions. This plan might take the form of a month-long prayer schedule or something as simple as a text message reminder to themselves to say "I love you" upon returning home to their spouse. Activities like storytelling and artistic expression (mentioned above as ways of synthesizing a personal vision) can also serve to reinforce significant decisions insofar as they approximate commonsense, everyday patterns of thought.

To the extent possible teachers should encourage learners to put their decisions into action (e.g., by participating in liturgy and service work), for nothing consolidates new ideas and images more effectively than acting upon them, especially in a consistent manner. Like spouses living out their wedding vows, we achieve a deeper knowledge of God and ourselves when we live into our decision for Jesus' vision. Indeed, what the reign of God is becomes most clear when we enact in our lives the vision into which Jesus draws us. As we saw in chapter 4, Jesus did not intend his parables as carriers of information about God and God's activity in the world; he intended them to coax us into an experience of God's ways, to convert our imagining to a God-like perspective, and to invite a decision to live life from that vision.

As a final note to this section, it is worth observing how being intentional about the role of decision in the learning process helps to ensure that we as teachers respect our students' autonomy. Besides obscuring alternative perspectives, constraining learners' decision-making is another way we can (intentionally or not) manipulate their thinking. In contrast with such coercive methods, when we explicitly invite learners to make their own decisions, it makes it less likely that they will be brainwashed with an opinion that they would not have chosen for themselves were they fully aware of its implications. It is never acceptable to manipulate students' thinking. However, it becomes particularly important for teachers to respect learners' autonomous decision-making when aiming to invite conversion to a new way of imagining. God does not convert us against our will, and neither should religious educators presume to do so.

HABITS OF A NEW INTERIORITY ACQUIRED THROUGH MOVEMENT 3

This book began from the premise that many Christians (and many others besides) today experience a mismatch between their capacity for making sense of reality and the demands of meaning-making and faith-making in postmodern society. In the past three chapters, I have been describing an approach to teaching and learning about faith that has helped many of my students to close that gap. Building upon the exercises of Movements 1 and 2 and the habits of imagining acquired therein, Movement 3 inculcates additional habits that mark the maturation of learners' meaning-making into a form that is more adequate to the challenges to faith and meaning endemic to postmodern culture.

The first set of habits pertain to learners' exercise of critical thinking. The distinguishing characteristic of critical meaning-makers is their capacity for reasoned judgment. They do not take things at face value but rather seek evidence and verification. Such critical thinking is indispensable for reflective persons living in post-Enlightenment, scientific society. They must be able to think rationally and flexibly about their own religious beliefs and practices (as well as about the surrounding culture) if their faith is to withstand the corrosive effect of the often skeptical attitudes of educators, learned authorities, and popular media toward faith and religion. For this reason, the exercises of Movement 3 are designed to affirm and strengthen learners' capacity to raise intelligent questions and make reasonable judgments based upon appropriate criteria.

As we saw above, empirical evidence and logical argumentation constitute essential but insufficient criteria for judgments that will lead to a life of abundance. In addition to wanting to know what is true and real, we long to belong and to know that our lives mean something. Therefore, those individuals who realize their humanity in its fullness tend also to judge images, beliefs, and practices upon their capacity to illuminate life experiences and to endow them with a sense of coherence and meaningfulness After a semester of reading the Bible and other Christian classics in conversation with both modern scientific research and the timeless questions of human existence, most students recognize that ancient religious texts can stand up to critical scrutiny and interrogation of a more existential sort. They leave with a humbler estimation of their own ability to answer life's questions and a higher estimation of the wisdom and power of these texts. They come to see that there is much more in these texts than they initially thought and, as such, are more inclined to return to these texts in the future (at least in their minds if not always to the books themselves). Through a semester of interrogating and learning from the texts in this manner, they have acquired a new set of criteria and a new habit for judging the truth and value of content presented to them. They have also gained in these classic texts and symbols a valuable set of resources for constructing meaning that many either previously rejected or never knew they had at their disposal.

Engaging classic texts in this critical manner tends to raise learners' awareness of not only new resources for making sense of the world but also personal capacities and responsibilities to which they had never paid attention. The judging exercises of Movement 3 help to make learners more aware of their meaning-making and the meanings they are appropriating, whether from their religious tradition, their local community, or the wider culture. Many students come to realize they have been appropriating meaning from their community, social media, and advertising in a passive manner. Some are shocked by the extent to which this is the case. Lightbulb moments like this wake learners up to the fact that they have a say in how they imagine reality. Exercises like those I incorporate into Movement 3 provide them with opportunities to act upon their awakened desire to assert greater control over their lives by making intentional judgements about what is true and valuable and clear-eyed decisions about what they want for themselves. Concretely, this heightened sense of personal responsibility might manifest in more critical and appreciative listening to Scripture in Sunday worship or a nightly praying of the Ignatian examen. This capacity for exercising greater existential self-responsibility (what Kegan and Baxter Magolda call "self-authorship") is a second major capacity developed in Movement 3.

At the same time, these exercises and experiences make learners more aware that their meaning-making and self-authoring is always an activity of co-authoring. They may not like it, but after watching Pariser's "filter bubble" TED Talk and reading Augustine's *Confessions*, they cannot deny that the technology and people they attach themselves to influence how they see the world. Furthermore, having reflected deeply on their own complicated lives and read radically different perspectives on life's big questions, many tend to be humbler about their need for guidance. For some, this realization is what prompts them to consider their religious tradition more seriously or to invest more intentionally in a relationship with God.

Third and finally, Movement 3 strengthens learners' capacity to synthesize a new vision when an old one has broken down. Although a Facebook post or Netflix documentary may occasionally inspire or guide us, the more common experience for many people—certainly for the majority of my students—is that the relentless hammering of diverse images and messages wears upon the hulls of our worldview and, in some cases, swamps us entirely. Given these conditions, contemporary Christians need to be able to repair and reconstruct their own worldview as necessary, a skillset that involves mental activities like those utilized in Movement 3.

It is clear to me that my students have benefited from my pedagogical decision to privilege symbols over (but not in opposition to) conceptual formulations. Dwelling within classic texts like the Bible and Dante's *Divine Comedy* and classic symbols like the reign of God, students discover a depth of meaning they seldom encounter in a culture of superficial, fleeting images. They also encounter persons and communities who have grappled with life's challenges and questions before them. They grapple with similar challenges and questions in dialogue with these texts, their classmates, and their teacher. And so, when their relationships and life plans fall apart, they can find themselves in Dante's or Dorothy Day's journey while they are working out a new story and vision for their lives. When they have trouble reconciling Christian doctrines with scientific findings or the prevailing opinions of progressive society, they can continue to find meaning and psychological support (if not always clear answers) in the story of the Prodigal Son, an icon of the Holy Trinity, or the Eucharist.

With the conclusion of this chapter, I have now described the three movements or sets of pedagogical habits that make up the SEE approach and the new habits of meaning-making that learners cultivate by engaging their own imaginings and the classic stories and symbols of the Christian tradition through this process. In the next and final chapter, I will offer some further clarifications concerning this approach and bring together the new habits described in the previous three chapters into a more organic portrait of how the new form of interiority these habits constitute leads to a fuller, more abundant life for Christians living in today's world. In the final pages, I will also describe how this approach to religious education might fit within a comprehensive response by Christian communities to postmodern challenges to faith and meaning-making.

chapter 7

SEE AND SEEING BEYOND

As this book draws to a close, let's recall why we set out on this exploration of an imagination-centered approach to religious education.

Two millennia ago, Jesus promised that by following him we would experience life in abundance. This life full of meaning, joy, and purpose is something we all desire. I first caught a glimpse of it during my college years, and I have spent my days pursuing it and working to share it with others ever since.

Although we all long for fullness of life, we mostly fall short of attaining it. As we saw in chapter 1, this shortcoming is primarily due to divisions within our hearts and minds that we all experience on account of sin. We succumb to our desires for many things that distract us from the one necessary thing, that is, from God, who is the true source of our life and happiness.

Every generation must confront this spiritual challenge. However, the "signs of the times" indicate that there are decidedly novel challenges preventing people today from experiencing the fullness of life. People are abandoning religious traditions at a historically unprecedented rate, and many of those who continue to identify with a religious community live lives that, outside of Sunday, appear unaffected by their religion. Young people especially—people like my student David whom I introduced at the beginning of the book—increasingly report feeling overwhelmed by life in today's world. Struggling to find meaning amidst the ups and downs of life, more and more people are succumbing to anxiety and depression. While the causes of disaffiliation and declining mental health are complex, I argued in chapter 2 that both phenomena find a common cause in a crisis of meaning afflicting postmodern society. As a result of the erosion of the

Christian imaginary in the West and the explosion of traditional sources of meaning more generally, many contemporary Christians are struggling to find meaning in their faith and in life in general.

Given this state of affairs, I argued (especially in chapter 3) that what is needed for Christians to reclaim the life of abundance that Jesus offers is a conversion of the imagination leading to new habits of meaning-making that are better suited to the mental demands of postmodern culture. Conversion is the fruit of the efforts not just of individuals but of entire communities working in countless ways to support their members in living the life of Christian discipleship. Religious education has its role to play in this work. If we religious educators are to play our role well in the current context, we must engage learners as meaning-makers and invite them to undergo a transformation in the way they imagine reality. In this book I have described how I have invited such transformation in my students and how other teachers might do likewise.

SEE AS AN EDUCATIONAL RESPONSE TO THE CRISIS OF MEANING

I have found much that is helpful to my students in the guidance of other religious educators and especially in the pedagogical example of Jesus. What is distinctive about the approach I have developed in this book is a particular concern for helping learners to cultivate the kinds of habits of meaning-making that will enable them to live meaningful, faithful lives in today's world. These habits, expressed in the most basic terms, constitute an ongoing process of (1) stimulating their imagination, (2) expanding their imagination, and (3) embracing new ways of imagining.

The SEE approach begins (Movement 1) by stimulating the mental activity by means of which learners imagine and make sense of reality. Exercises for activating learners' imagining include:

- presenting a focusing image (e.g., a piece of artwork, a song, a video) that elicits learners' own mental images, and

- posing evocative questions that invite learners to reflect upon their mental images.

In Movement 2, teachers invite learners to expand their imagining by engaging them with Jesus' vision of the reign of God and the stories, symbols, rituals, and practices that flow from that vision. This expansion of the imagination typically happens by means of a double movement that involves:

- disrupting limiting ways of imagining through self-examination and engaging provocative classic symbols, and

- exploring the deep meaning carried in these classic Christian symbols.

In Movement 3, teachers invite learners to embrace a new and more adequate manner of imagining inspired by their engagement with Jesus' vision of the reign of God. I have found that I can best help my students to forge a new vision for their lives when I:

- support them psychologically and emotionally during the transition,

- invite them to make their own informed judgments about the veracity as well as the meaningfulness of images presented to them, and

- provide opportunities for them to make concrete decisions about whether and how they will pursue their new vision.

Reflecting on my teaching over the years, I recognize that I became more effective in promoting these habits in my students as this approach became less a matter of theory and more a matter of habit for me. It is therefore not incidental that I describe the SEE approach as a set of pedagogical habits rather than a set of techniques. Describing SEE as a process or a set of pedagogical habits emphasizes the limitations and conditions for success of such a pedagogical approach. Because any fundamental change to the way we see things requires time and reinforcement, the effectiveness of the approach depends upon teachers employing it in a habitual, consistent manner rather than on an occasional basis. Besides, even where it succeeds in achieving its aims, an approach to religious education like SEE is insufficient by itself to transform a person's life. SEE is an invitation to the fullness of life; it is not the fullness of life itself.

TO *SEE* IS TO BEGIN EVER ANEW

The primary reason that so many people are failing to find meaning in the Christian tradition today is not that they lack the requisite knowledge. The problem goes deeper than that. More fundamentally, many contemporary people lack a coherent framework for making sense of their lives, including their religious traditions. The issue is at root a profound crisis of meaning.

An adequate educational response to this state of affairs must, therefore, go beyond transmitting beliefs and doctrines as conceptual formulations to transforming the means by which people imagine and construct meaning. Transforming meaning frameworks is arduous work. We do not develop habits that generate and sustain our worldview by cognizing an idea once or twice, but by returning to our master images over and over, by meditating upon them and dwelling in them. For this reason, I am not optimistic about the prospects of any approach to religious education—including the SEE approach—restoring the meaningfulness of the Christian tradition unless it repeatedly engages learners in something like the three movements I have described in this book. Even though I do see clear gains in some of my university students over the course of a semester, I recognize that these gains are more limited than they could be if we had more time together.

Elementary and high school religious education and parish or congregational faith formation programs present more favorable circumstances for the SEE approach, insofar as learners often return year after year. In such programs, learners are able to revisit core Christian symbols and teachings once or several times per year or per meeting period.[1] Repeatedly returning to these core symbols does not mean rehashing the same content in the same way year after year. Rather, returning to the same topics repeatedly over time allows for deepening and nuancing of learners' understanding of them, a dynamic illustrated by an upward spiral as opposed to a one-dimensional loop.[2] Given the inexhaustible depth of their meaning, classic Christian symbols invite us to dive ever deeper into their depths. Speaking from a developmental perspective, high school students are capable of thinking about the stories of Scripture in a more sophisticated way than second graders and, consequently, of discovering new meanings. Adults are capable of still more sophisticated thinking. At its best, Christian religious education challenges learners to deepen their learning continuously to the extent possible for their level of cognitive development and reinforces the value of lifelong learning, especially when it comes to entering ever more deeply into the mystery of God.

---

1. See chapter 5 for a suggestive list of these symbols.
2. See Bruner, *Process of Education*, on this "spiraling" approach to curriculum.

DIVERSE APPLICATIONS OF THE *SEE* APPROACH

The SEE approach emerged out of my efforts to help my (mostly college) students meet the mental challenges they encounter in the postmodern world. In that regard, the primary aim of SEE is to promote the conversion of learners' imagining to a post-critical form of Christian meaning-making. Yet the usefulness of the SEE approach extends far beyond a limited audience of adult learners. Although SEE has the capacity to promote a new form of interiority, it serves just as well to invite conversion to the reign of God at a pre-critical level such as that discussed in chapter 2.

A teacher with this more fundamental goal will not use all the exercises described in chapters 5 and 6 (e.g., critical self-examination of learners' meaning-making or critically interpreting Christian symbols), but the general movements still apply. Facilitating any form of conversion or radical transformation necessarily involves tapping into learners' accustomed ways of imagining (Movement 1), presenting a more expansive way of imagining (Movement 2), and then inviting learners to make that more expansive vision their own (Movement 3). In sum, SEE can promote conversion to the reign of God in learners of all developmental levels.

The SEE approach can also serve more traditional aims of religious education like improving learners' understanding of Christian teachings because, besides its transformative potential, this approach is just plain good pedagogy. It is designed so that its basic movements accord with the natural dynamics of how human beings learn and construct meaning, making the process suitable for nearly all learners.[3] This imagination-focused pedagogy is appropriate for young children since the prominent use of images is more likely to attract and hold their attention than, for example, an approach built around definitions and doctrines.[4] Yet it is no less appropriate for adults in whose cognitional processes images continue to fulfill essential functions.

Of course, as with any pedagogical approach, the effectiveness of this process depends to some degree upon the teacher offering differentiated instruction according to the needs of learners. For young learners, teachers should spend more time examining images, telling stories, and undertaking

---

3. Like all pedagogical approaches, this one, too, requires appropriate adaptations for learners with cognitive disabilities.

4. Again, I reiterate that there is no conflict between teaching symbols and teaching doctrines. Doctrines play a crucial role in religious education. The issue here is how and when the teacher employs symbols and doctrines.

artistic projects, thereby respecting the limits of children's short attention spans and concrete manner of thinking. Adults, by contrast, typically have longer attention spans and the ability to engage in abstract thought. In their case, learning experiences allow for more sophisticated questions and for more nuance and precision in discussing Christian teachings. As with any educational approach, the SEE approach will be most effective when teachers adapt it to the learners' social context and cultural background, emotional maturity, and comfort level with one another.

The reader might reasonably question whether teachers who have themselves not yet attained a post-critical form of consciousness are able to use this approach. In response I would reiterate that the SEE approach can be useful in many ways that do not involve engaging learners in exercises for promoting post-critical meaning-making (for example, when using SEE with children) and, therefore, do not require teachers to possess post-critical capacities. It is true that our religious communities will benefit if more religious educators are able to model post-critical Christian imagining and facilitate learners' growth into such meaning-making themselves. Yet it is not the case that all Christians or all religious educators need to develop post-critical capacities in order to live fulfilled lives in today's world. As more and more Christians move into post-critical consciousness, that consciousness will gradually pervade the culture of Christian communities through their presence and the language, customs, and artistic expression emanating from these post-critical Christians. Once the culture reaches that tipping point, the post-critical meanings and habits of meaning-making embedded in that culture will support pre-critical and critical meaning-makers in their meaning-making, as happens whenever some new development is gradually absorbed into the mainstream culture. We have not yet reached such a critical mass of post-critical Christians in our communities. Until we do, many people will continue to struggle to make sense of the postmodern world, and individual development of post-critical capacities will remain an urgent task for religious education.

THE FRUIT OF THE *SEE* APPROACH: A NEW WAY OF SEEING AND LIVING

I have peppered the preceding chapters with anecdotes and examples of how engaging in the SEE process has enhanced my students' capacity for making sense of their lives. I have also identified the specific new habits of meaning-making cultivated by each of the three movements. However, the success of an approach like SEE cannot be evaluated merely by marking off a checklist of skills or competencies developed. The point of this approach is to help contemporary Christians make sense of and flourish in today's world. For that reason it is important here at the end of the book to offer a more holistic picture of how a pedagogical approach like SEE can transform learners' lives.

Developing a post-critical form of meaning-making does not mean having it all figured out. No student has ever declared to me at the end of the semester that they had arrived at the definitive answers to all life's big questions. What some do report is feeling less anxious and better able to make sense of things than they were before. Such is the benefit of being anchored to something stable in the midst of life's vicissitudes. When my students and others achieve a greater degree of equanimity, it is often because their imaginative engagement with the Christian tradition has fortified and transformed their master symbols of God, world, self, and other.[5] Anchoring them are an image of God as Love incarnate in the person of Jesus Christ, an image of the world as the ground of the inbreaking of God's reign, and images of self and other alike as beloved children of God (or some variation thereof).

Cultivating this new form of interiority does not somehow lift Christians above the challenges of postmodern life. At semester's end, many questions still linger for my students concerning who God is, why the world is the way it is, and how they should live their lives. Still, these core Christian symbols can provide an abiding sense of identity and purpose in the world. Grounding themselves in these revealed symbols enables Christians to respond to life's challenges with greater adaptability and resilience and in a way that is authentically Christian. When some day in the future my students break up with a significant other, fail an exam, or get laid off at work, many will be able to maintain a degree of peace and acceptance in knowing that they are a beloved child of God, even if they do not know whether and when they will find romantic love again, complete the degree, or find another job.

Engaging classic Christian symbols in the classroom often leads to students engaging Christian texts, rituals, and practices more seriously outside of the classroom. By exploring these classics intentionally in the

---

5. See Astin et al., *Cultivating the Spirit*, 49–62 for a corroborating discussion of equanimity, what promotes it, and why it correlates strongly with quality of life.

class (perhaps for the first time in their lives), learners encounter a depth of meaning that sheds light upon their experiences of suffering, joy, and relationship. Once they get a taste, they want more. Some will begin reading the Bible at home or return to Sunday worship or just attend their regular worship services more attentively. They do so of their own accord and on their own terms because they now detect potential value and meaning in these practices. They do so well aware that these rituals can devolve into superstition and formalism at the hands of people—perhaps themselves at an earlier stage—who approach them uncritically. However, they also recognize their need for the powerful, life-giving meaning that symbols and ritual bestow, and so they give themselves over to these rituals—not naively, not uncritically, but with a sense of openness nonetheless.

Of course, post-critical meaning-making is not merely a matter of *what* the Christian imagines but also of *how* they imagine. A crucial dimension of this "how" that distinguishes post-critical meaning-makers is their high level of self-awareness. One clear indicator that my students are growing into a new form of interiority is that they talk about meaning as something they actively construct rather than as a given. Another is that they talk about the influence of media, advertising, and other people over how they perceive and make sense of things. This is a major area of growth for many of my students in the time that we are together. When they first arrive at the start of the semester, many are relatively unreflective about how the music and videos they choose to consume shape their view of reality. Developing this heightened self-awareness makes them less susceptible to unconsciously internalizing the messages of advertisers and other third parties. They also feel less overwhelmed by the rapid pace of cultural and technological change and the constant bombardment of images and messages in social media and popular culture because they have a more autonomous, stable sense of self. They exercise greater responsibility for their own imagining, for instance, by making more intentional decisions about when and how they consume content and use social media. Some quit Facebook, Twitter, and/or Instagram altogether. Some persist in the devotional habits I introduce in class, like the daily examen, *lectio divina*, or the Jesus Prayer in order to immerse themselves more fully in the Christian imaginary.

By the end of the semester, a few will even demonstrate an awareness of their inescapable dependence upon other people, society, and perhaps even God for constructing a meaningful life. In other words, they recognize that, for even the most self-aware among us, our self-authoring is always a co-authoring of meaning. Those who arrive at this realization are consequently even further disposed to return to the classic symbols, stories, and rituals of the Christian tradition in their ongoing search for meaning.

Because SEE helps learners to strengthen and balance their critical thinking with an expanded symbolic consciousness, they are better able to cope with tensions they experience in contemporary educational and social contexts. At the start of the academic year, there is always a mix of students who, on the one side, have never applied critical methods of inquiry to their religious beliefs and those who, on the other, scoff at theological inquiry and religious ways of thinking. Throughout the semester, I challenge everyone in the class to take religious texts and symbols seriously, to consider how they might illuminate their own experiences, but also to examine them critically, to ask challenging questions and engage these classics in dialogue with other areas of learning and study. With time and practice, pre-critical students become less intimidated by professors who employ critical methods or by scientific findings that bear upon their religious convictions. Both pre-critical and critical students become better able to recognize the narrowness of rationalist critiques of religion and the deeper meaning that resides within religious classics and revealed symbols.

I also see the difference in how my students relate to one another and to the one who is "other." Because post-critical meaning-makers demonstrate more flexibility in their thinking, they tend to be more willing and better able to abide the tensions that frequently arise in pluralistic societies. Pre-critical meaning-makers tend to be so constrained by their naive, sometimes fundamentalist thinking that they cannot enter into the perspective of someone from a different culture or tradition. Critical meaning-makers' suspicion of universalizing truth claims can prevent them from seriously considering the truthfulness or meaningfulness of another's perspective, particularly if that perspective is a religious one. This mindset characterizes the vast majority of my students, who are at the same time highly tolerant of differing perspectives and so averse to passing judgment on any religious perspective that they seem unable to commit themselves to any particular framework. They merely drift upon the surface of a sea of diverse perspectives. By contrast, my students who are able to grow beyond a critical form of consciousness are rooted firmly enough in their master symbols that they have the calm confidence needed to engage people of differing perspectives in a manner that is genuinely open and appreciative yet not uncritical. They do not perceive difference as threatening (or at least it seems less so). To the contrary, such students tend to listen to others with more genuine interest, ask better questions, and be more open to revising their own thinking.

This openness and curiosity is perhaps one reason for the attractiveness of post-critical people. When I encounter students and others who are growing into this new form of interiority, I am often struck by an uncommon liveliness, depth, and/or sense of purpose that stands in stark contrast to the superficiality and emptiness that characterizes the lives of so many other people I meet on a daily basis. By entering more deeply into their own interiority and by recovering the meaningfulness of faith on the other side of criticism, these post-critical Christians have recovered a felt sense of God's love and presence in their lives that a generation of skeptical, excarnated Christians has lost.

To pull all this together in an image, people who have grown into this new form of interiority embody a greater degree of stability, but it is more like the stability of a sailboat with a deep keel than that of a stone fortress. Their stability and equanimity is in their depth and their drive rather than in any inflexibility. They need not have all the answers because they have come into contact with a tradition (and perhaps a Person) who offers profound meaning for their life. They have glimpsed a vision that gives them a sense of direction and pulls them forward into their future. And, although they continue to grapple with the same challenges we all face in pluralistic, media-saturated postmodern societies, they are daily living into that vision and drawing nearer to the Source of the life of meaning and fullness for which they yearn.

Of course not all post-critical meaning-makers return to the religion of their youth. Not all of my students become devoted church-goers by semester's end. A natural consequence of growth into a more flexible form of faith- and meaning-making is that such people chart varied courses on their journey to God. Recovering an appreciation of religious meanings and practices is a hallmark of this new form of interiority, but whether or not any given individual will actually enter or reenter a particular religious community depends equally upon the presence and attractiveness of an invitation—from teachers, mentors, clergy, friends—to enter.

What I describe above is a patchwork of stories. Different people's individual stories reflect certain aspects of this portrait more than others. For the sake of clarity I have described the journey to a new interiority in terms of three distinct forms of meaning-making, but the reality of human development is much messier. Development from one form to another can be slow and uneven. People manifest some characteristics of post-critical meaning-making while persisting in some critical tendencies. Backsliding can occur. Still, a person growing into this new form of interiority will inevitably see certain new capacities: an enhanced awareness of how they construct meaning, greater control over their meaning-making, and the union of critical and symbolic thinking.

Since implementing the SEE approach, I regularly witness the early signs of such growth in my students. However, these early signs are only a beginning. In order for these first sproutlings to blossom into the total transformation of learners' imagining and living, they will need to find support and nourishment within a community constituted by a robust Christian imaginary and way of life flowing from that vision. Here we press up against the limits of the SEE approach because this is more than an approach to religious education can offer. The approach I have described in this book is an invitation to "come and see." It will take the collective efforts of the entire church community to support the ongoing work of transformation in the people who respond to this invitation. The more consistently our faith communities are able to provide this kind of support to their members, the more likely it becomes that people will be able to meet the mental challenges of the day and the less likely they are to lose their sense of the meaningfulness of their faith and of life as a whole.

BEYOND *SEE*: A CONCLUDING VISION AND INVITATION

Entering into and embracing Jesus' vision of the reign of God, we begin to see how our lives must change. Nothing less than total transformation will suffice. Jesus makes this point emphatically when he commands us to love God with all our heart, mind, soul, and strength, and our neighbor as ourselves (Luke 10:27; cf. Matt 22:37). Jesus' words at once highlight the complexity of the human person and the simplicity of the solution to overcoming our internal and external divisions and living full, meaningful lives: We must hold nothing back and seek after God and God's reign with everything we've got.

Applying this principle to the mission of the church, it is clear that the work of promoting conversion will require the support of the entire Christian community and incorporate a variety of approaches, of which the present project constitutes just one. For that reason, it is important to situate the pedagogical approach I have presented in this book within this wider network of efforts. The primary aim of SEE is to invite a conversion of the imagination. That is where Jesus began so often, and it has been my experience as a teacher that beginning in this way opens up many possibilities. Still, converting the imagination is only the beginning of a full conversion to the reign of God. It therefore seems suitable to conclude this book by (a) pointing to the work of other religious educators, scholars, and leaders that contributes to the deepening of conversion in its different dimensions and (b) inviting readers to think about how their work in their diverse ministries might help contemporary people live abundantly amidst the challenges and opportunities of postmodern culture.

Converting the Mind—Religious Education

Despite declining enrollments and attendance, formal educational settings like parochial schools, parish and congregational religious education programs, and Christian colleges and universities continue to provide some of our best opportunities to prepare students to live with "the mind of Christ" in today's world (1 Cor 2:16, NRSV). Both Paul's call to be transformed by the renewal of the mind (*nous*) and Jesus' command to love God with all one's mind (*dianoia*) evoke a more holistic conception of the human mind and a more radical notion of its transformation. This more expansive conception of the mind and its transformation has been operative in my discussion of imagination, meaning-making, and teaching throughout this book. I have argued that restoring the meaningfulness of the faith in the lives of postmodern people will require recognizing faith as an activity of meaning-making and teaching the faith in a way that invites learners to undergo a transformation in their meaning-making. This sort of transformation involves not merely thinking about Christ but, more profoundly, seeing reality through his eyes.

In undertaking this project, I recognize similar efforts by other religious educators to transform the minds of learners. I see the "biblical worldview" approach to Christian education—currently most common within Protestant communities—as a step in this direction.[6] There is great promise in the work of certain European religious educators who have developed pedagogies that support students in intentionally developing their own

6. Cf. van der Kooij et al., "'Worldview,'" 223.

worldviews.[7] Particularly if conducted in a sustained manner that forms learners in the skills and habits required for life-long meaning construction, this latter approach has the potential to bring about enduring, life-changing transformation in the lives of students.

Here in the United States, two religious educators have been particularly helpful to me in thinking about how to transform the minds of my students. First, Sharon Daloz Parks in her book *Big Questions, Worthy Dreams* offers helpful guidance for how mentoring communities can support faith education that is not only informative but also facilitates the kind of personal transformation needed to maintain faith in a postmodern culture. One way that faith communities can foster transformation is by instilling the habits of mind needed to make meaning of faith and life in the postmodern world. Among these habits Parks includes genuine dialogue, critical thought, connective-holistic awareness, and the contemplative mind.[8] When Parks writes about critical thought, she means something akin to the post-critical self-awareness I have described. Her description of the "contemplative mind" also resonates with the central themes of the present book.[9]

Thomas Groome, another religious educator who aspires to the holistic transformation of the learner, similarly emphasizes the importance of teaching learners to think "critically and contemplatively" for themselves.[10] Groome's "shared Christian praxis" approach (SCP) promotes critical and contemplative thinking by structuring the learning event in five movements that invite learners to put their own questions, experiences, and insights into dialogue with the Christian "Story and Vision" and ultimately to make an informed personal decision for faith. Shared praxis thus offers religious educators a practicable model for how to facilitate learners' integration of the Christian Story/Vision with their personal stories and visions and nurture a faith that entails not merely impersonal assent to propositions but a transformed way of life.

My own teaching has been greatly influenced by Groome's SCP. Many of the exercises of SCP have proven valuable in my efforts to respond to

---

7. See van der Kooij et al., "'Worldview,'" 224, 226; Pollefeyt, "Difference Matters"; Mulder and van den Berg, *Learning for Life*.

8. Daloz Parks, *Big Questions, Worthy Dreams*, 142.

9. Although we address similar concerns, Parks's response focuses on the role of mentoring while mine focuses on that of teaching in traditional educational settings.

10. Groome, *Sharing Faith*, 94.

the new challenges to faith and meaning-making presented by postmodern culture. Nonetheless, Groome developed his approach in an earlier time and with different concerns in mind, and so I have found it necessary to go beyond SCP by bringing the work of meaning construction to the fore of my teaching and developing exercises that specifically promote a post-critical form of meaning-making.[11]

With these models of transformative religious education in mind, I invite religious educators to consider the following as they envision ways of better preparing learners for faithful living in postmodern society:

- What truly motivates and guides the work of our Christian educational institutions? Are we allowing current trends in education, rival institutions, and the wider culture to distract us from goals more central to the mission of the church?

- To what extent do our learning outcomes and assessments reflect a commitment to helping our students cultivate not just an intellectual understanding of the tenets of faith but the very mind of Christ?

- How well do our curricula and teaching respond to the changing demands of living faithfully in contemporary culture?

Converting the Soul—Liturgy and Art

The term "soul" or "psyche" carries various connotations, but in the New Testament it refers primarily to the animating force within the human being. Operating within the realm of modern psychology, Robert Kegan relates this "irreducible" and "primary human motion" to the activity of meaning-making.[12] As we saw in chapter 2, our sensing and imagining are even more foundational to our meaning-making than our concepts and reasonings.[13]

11. Although Groome by and large does not frame his project as a corrective to a particular educational exigency, his earlier writing evinces a concern to correct overly cognitive, knowledge-focused models of Christian religious education (see Groome, *Christian Religious Education*, 12; *Sharing Faith*, 2). Groome's most recent book does acknowledge the challenges of postmodernity more explicitly, but it does not offer a substantively different approach than that presented in earlier works (see Groome, *Will There Be Faith?*, 1–2).

12. Kegan, *Evolving Self*, 19.

13. Following New Testament usage, the heart rather than soul would actually correspond more precisely to the origin of thoughts and mental images. However, to avoid inevitable confusion, I am conceding to modern usage of these terms in which the psyche

It follows that Christian formation, if it is to transform people in the core of their being, will touch not only the surface level of their discursive thinking but also the deeper levels of their imagining.[14]

Much fine work has already been done toward this end. One example is the work of James K. A. Smith, who clearly recognizes the importance of forming Christians' affectivity and imaginations. In his cultural liturgies trilogy, Smith suggests that in order to counter the mis-formation of "secular liturgies" in the surrounding culture (e.g., compulsive consumption, sporting events, Hollywood movies), Christian communities need to pay more attention to people's desiring and imagining and, more specifically, engage in liturgies that form and transform Christians' habits of desiring and imagining.[15]

In addition to liturgy, art and literature present valuable resources to Christian communities seeking to facilitate transformation of the psyche.[16] In his beautiful book *Rekindling the Christic Imagination*, Robert Imbelli follows the aesthetic approach of theologians like Hans Urs van Balthasar and Benedict XVI in responding to the eclipse of Christ and the resulting fragmentation in the modern Catholic Church. Each of the book's four chapters meditates upon a piece of Christian art in an effort to evoke a Mystery that has faded from many Christians' imaginations. As a practitioner-scholar, Eileen Daily has provided more practical guidance for how religious educators can use religious artwork to transform the imaginations of students in parish and school settings.[17] In his book *The Wounded Angel*, theologian Paul Lakeland testifies to how engaging students with serious works of fiction like Flannery O'Connor's *Wise Blood* and Graham Greene's *The Power and the Glory* not only engages students as little else does but also restores a sense of the meaning of the whole and of the holy that so many young people lack today. All of the above points to the importance of Christian artists. If our Christian communities are serious about the

---

is more commonly ascribed the sensitive and imaginative capacities.

14. Paul Ricoeur suggests as much when he writes that "every real conversion is first a revolution at the level of our directive images" (Ricoeur, *History and Truth*, 127).

15. Smith, *Desiring the Kingdom*, 25. Timothy O'Malley presents a similar but distinctively Catholic liturgical response to these problems in his book *Liturgy and the New Evangelization*.

16. Not incidentally, at the end of *A Secular Age*, Charles Taylor points to the "subtler languages" of poetry, art, and story as the way out of the secularized, immanent frame (732).

17. Daily, *Beyond the Written Word*; cf. Starratt, "Education with a Sense of Wonder."

mission of inviting conversion and initiating people into the fullness of the Christian life, we need to lift up the vocation of artist and support a new generation of Dantes and Flannery O'Connors, individuals who possess a gift for stirring our imaginations.[18]

Formal religious education, too, has a role to play in converting imaginations. Although Christian art, film, and literature have the potential to do this in their own right, formal religious education offers an ideal environment for the kind of reflection needed to deepen and refine the insights and inspirations that arise in personal experience or encounters with religious art and to work out the concrete implications of conversion. Movie theaters and liturgical settings do not allow as easily for this kind of in-depth reflection. My hope is that this book has provided one model for how religious educators might go about this work of transforming imaginations.

Having briefly surveyed some current efforts to promote conversion through liturgy, art, and literature, I invite Christian leaders to reflect on how we can extend these efforts. More specifically, I invite readers to consider the following:

- How might Christian communities lift up and nurture artistic vocations?

- How might we better incorporate high-quality art, literature, music, and film throughout the life of our faith communities?[19]

- What new media are presenting novel opportunities for engaging the imaginations of contemporary people?

Converting Our Living—Christian Practices

More frequent contact with Christian images in the classroom, worship, devotional study, and elsewhere will help to attract and stimulate people's imagining. If that engagement is to amount to anything more than a momentary stimulation of the imagination (of which contemporary people experience no shortage), people must find a means to deepen the vision

---

18. Christopher Pramuk has done precisely this in his creative book *The Artist Alive*.

19. The Catholic Christian tradition very much embraces art and visual representation, but this is not always the case in different Protestant denominations or in Islam. I invite leaders in these traditions to consider if and how their faith communities might make use of art in ways that are authentic to their traditions.

these images intimate, to absorb it into their bones. Christian liturgy and practices offer such a means.

When arguing for the need for Christian communities to take liturgy seriously, James Smith has in mind not only church worship but also habit-forming practices like daily prayer, devotional reading, hospitality, and fasting.[20] Sharon Parks suggests that cultivating life-giving practices is one crucial way that mentoring communities support young people's faith and meaning-making. Jane Regan develops this idea in greater depth in her book *Where Two or Three Are Gathered*, which explores the dynamics of parish "communities of practice." Therein Regan presents a vision of how the different parish committees and groups—parish councils, liturgy committees, social justice committees, catechists, choirs, etc.—can renew and transform individuals and the community through practices of hospitality, conversation, followership, and discernment.

Reaching back into the Christian tradition and into contemporary communities, Craig Dykstra and Dorothy Bass have found that certain practices have consistently helped individuals and communities to experience life as meaningful and whole.[21] By "Christian practices" they mean patterns of action that we learn and perform in community, that involve us in God's activity in the world, and that address fundamental human needs. These include honoring the body, household economics, keeping Sabbath, forgiveness, healing, and dying well in addition to several practices already mentioned by other authors above.[22] These simple yet deeply significant practices provide the brick and mortar needed to construct a thoroughly Christian way of life.

Taking a cue from this body of work, Christian leaders might consider:

- How might our faith communities implement these scholars' proposals to enact Jesus' vision of the reign of God in liturgies that fully engage worshipers hearts, minds, imaginations, and bodies?

- What "secular liturgies" are currently shaping our desiring and imagining? To what effect?

20. Smith employs an expansive concept of liturgies, which he describes as a certain species of practice. See chapter 5 of Smith, *Desiring the Kingdom*.

21. To say that practices have consistently nourished the life of Christian communities and individuals is not to say that practices cannot be corrupted or produce negative effects. For a critique of overly optimistic appraisals of Christian practices, see Winner, *Dangers of Christian Practice*.

22. Bass, *Practicing Our Faith*.

- Are there customs and habits embedded in our faith communities that actually work counter to conversion to the reign of God?

- What are the embodied practices that suit the environment, culture, people, opportunities, and needs of our local communities?

Converting the Heart—Prayer and Community

Inviting and supporting conversion through religious education, art, liturgy, and practices presumes a supportive community. In chapter 6, I underscored the crucial role supportive community and relationships play in times of difficult transition. When our accustomed ways of making sense of things have fallen away and our world has reverted into chaos, we cling to the people who care about us. It is also the living disciples around us who put before our eyes the most powerful images of the Christian life in all its fullness.

Here again I return to the work of Sharon Daloz Parks, for no one has written more compellingly about the nurturing power of community in faith formation than she. Like myself, Parks draws upon developmental psychology in order to understand the struggles of today's young people. In *Big Questions, Worthy Dreams*, she explains that, while young adulthood is always a challenging transitional period, the forces of globalization and the weakening of traditional resources for making sense of life (like institutional religion) have made it more necessary than ever to support young adults in growing into more mature forms of meaning-making. Because we human beings desire nothing more than to belong, the communities to which we belong exercise tremendous influence over our meaning-making. Recognizing this powerful influence, Parks argues that we need to create mentoring communities that support young people in meeting the mental challenges of the day. The communities that do this best, she suggests, provide certain resources, including "a network of belonging, big enough questions, encounters with otherness, important habits of mind, worthy dreams, access to key images, concepts (content), and practices."[23]

Thinking about the role of community in promoting conversion, Christian leaders might consider:

- To what extent do our faith communities expect, welcome, and support conversion? What concrete supports are in place for people in

23. Daloz Parks, *Big Questions, Worthy Dreams*, 135.

transition (e.g., mentors in faith, spiritual direction, small faith communities)? Are people aware of these resources?

- Are we consistently able to identify and train people with charisms for spiritual accompaniment and mentoring?

- Given that we cannot truly love God without loving our neighbor (1 John 4:7–12), how do we help people to enter into communion with others?

Of course, all human community is but a reflection and a foretaste of the deeper union to which we are called with God. In this sense, prayer is the goal towards which this entire book and all the efforts of the church lead. I have described the SEE approach as a pedagogy of invitation. It is an invitation to conversion, which is to say it is an invitation to turn away from all that distracts and distorts our desiring and imagining and to enter more deeply into relationship with Christ. Although Jesus as a classic symbol attracts and fascinates, the SEE approach invites learners to come to know him as more than a symbol. The hope is that they will come to know Jesus intimately as a real person in whose love they experience the fullness of life.

Such intimacy of communion goes beyond the limits of religious education, even beyond the limits of the imagination. The wisdom of the Christian tradition is that we can only go so far guided by our eyes and imaginations. Saint Paul reminded the early Christians that "we walk by faith, not by sight" (2 Cor 5:7, NRSV). Early in his ministry Jesus used stories and images to invite his audiences to "come and see" how God's reign was breaking into the world, but after his resurrection he warned his followers about clinging to him (John 20:17) and then later ascended "out of their sight" (Acts 1:9, NRSV). We need imagination and images in the spiritual life. They provide the sign posts that lead us out of the wilderness and into the promised land. But, as Saint Augustine observed, we must not become beholden to images lest they become idolatrous distractions from our actual destination, from the One to whom they point.[24]

So beyond imagination-centered pedagogy, beyond Christian artwork, beyond Christian mentors and role models, there is prayer. More specifically, great saints like Teresa of Avila and John of the Cross have pointed to imageless, wordless attentiveness to God's loving presence as the goal of the Christian life. In our own time, spiritual guides like Thomas Merton, Thomas Keating, and Ronald Rolheiser have sought to recover

---

24. Augustine, *On Christian Doctrine*, I.4.

this tradition of contemplative prayer that transformed and nurtured the interior life of past generations of Christians.[25]

Setting our sights and our hearts on this goal of union with God, I invite Christian leaders to reflect on the following:

- How well do the various activities and ministries in our communities of faith lead members to prayerful encounter with God?

- Have any of our activities, policies, or behaviors become a distraction from prayer?

- In our classes, meetings, gatherings, and events, do we genuinely open ourselves to God's loving presence through our prayer, or do we pray in a merely perfunctory manner?

- How can we provide people with the space and guidance they need to enter God's presence in a distracted world?

- What opportunities for new modes of prayer have recent cultural and technological developments opened up?

The present is a moment of considerable challenges but also of great opportunity. Many times in the two thousand-year history of Christianity major cultural changes have forced Christians to reexamine their beliefs and behaviors and thereby catalyzed renewal and reinvigoration of the people of God. I believe that recent shifts in our culture are inviting Christians to a new manner of envisioning and living their lives, one firmly rooted in the life-giving symbols of the Christian faith and yet flexible enough to adapt to the constant influx of new information and cultural change that defines postmodern society.

If my own experience and much supporting research is any indication, religious education can play an important role in supporting contemporary people as they move into this new way of seeing and living. I invite other Christian educators to try for themselves the approach I have described in this book, to adapt it and improve upon it. I also hope that religious educators from other traditions will find something in this book that spurs their thinking about how best to respond to today's challenges to faith and meaning. Finally, I invite leaders of all kinds in our religious communities to imagine complementary ways of inviting conversion in contemporary persons' thinking, desiring, and living, perhaps pursuing some of the paths

---

25. For example, see Merton, *New Seeds of Contemplation*; Keating, *Open Mind, Open Heart*; Rolheiser, *Shattered Lantern*.

laid out above. May we, like the Christians of the early church, work together so that our students, parishioners, families, communities, and all people can enter into the life of abundance that God desires for us "so that our joy may be complete" (1 John 1:4, NRSV).

BIBLIOGRAPHY

Ambrose, Susan A., et al. *How Learning Works: Seven Research-Based Principles for Smart Teaching*. San Francisco: Jossey-Bass, 2010.

Antonovsky, Aaron. *Unraveling the Mystery of Health: How People Manage Stress and Stay Well*. San Francisco: Jossey-Bass, 1987.

Aquinas, Thomas. *De Veritate*. Translated by Robert W. Mulligan. Chicago: Henry Regnery, 1952. Online. http://dhspriory.org/thomas/english/QDdeVer2.htm.

Astin, Alexander W., et al. *Cultivating the Spirit: How College Can Enhance Students' Inner Lives*. San Francisco: Jossey-Bass, 2010.

Augustine, Saint. *Confessions*. Translated by Henry Chadwick. New York: Oxford University Press, 1998.

———. *On Christian Doctrine*. Translated by D. W. Robertons Jr. Upper Saddle River, NJ: Prentice Hall, 1958.

Barbezat, Daniel P., and Mirabai Bush. *Contemplative Practices in Higher Education: Powerful Methods to Transform Teaching and Learning*. San Francisco: Jossey-Bass, 2014.

Barryman, Jerome. *Godly Play: A Way of Religious Education*. San Francisco: HarperSanFrancisco, 1991.

Bass, Dorothy C., ed. *Practicing Our Faith: A Way of Life for a Searching People*. San Francisco: Jossey-Bass, 1997.

Baxter Magolda, Marcia B. *Making Their Own Way: Narratives for Transforming Higher Education to Promote Self-development*. Sterling, VA: Stylus, 2001.

Baxter Magolda, Marcia B., and Patricia M. King. *Learning Partnerships: Theory and Models of Practice to Educate for Self-authorship*. Sterling, VA: Stylus, 2004.

Bell, Rob. *Velvet Elvis: Repainting the Christian Faith*. New York: HarperCollins, 2005.

Benedict XVI. "Deus Caritas Est." Encyclical Letter, December 25, 2005. Online. http://www.vatican.va/content/benedict-xvi/en/encyclicals/documents/hf_ben-xvi_enc_20051225_deus-caritas-est.html.

———. "Verbum Domini: On the Word of God in the Life and Mission of the Church." Apostolic Exhortation, September 30, 2010. Online. http://w2.vatican.va/content/benedictxvi/en/apost_exhortations/documents/hf_ben-xvi_exh_20100930_verbum-domini.html.

Berger, Peter L. *The Sacred Canopy: Elements of a Sociological Theory of Religion.* Garden City, NY: Anchor, 1969.

Bohlmeijer, Ernst, et al. "The Effects of Mindfulness-based Stress Reduction Therapy on Mental Health of Adults with a Chronic Medical Disease: A Meta-analysis." *Journal of Psychosomatic Research* 68 (2010) 539–44.

Bowman, Nicholas A., and Jenny L. Small. "Exploring a Hidden Form of Minority Status: College Students' Religious Affiliation and Well-being." *Journal of College Student Development* 53 (2012) 491–509.

Brueggemann, Walter. *Finally Comes the Poet: Daring Speech for Proclamation.* Minneapolis: Fortress, 1989.

Bruner, Jerome S. *The Process of Education.* Revised ed. Cambridge, MA: Harvard University Press, 2009.

Carlson, Kurt A., and Suzanne B. Shu. "When Three Charms But Four Alarms: Identifying the Optimal Number of Claims in Persuasion Settings." *SSRN*, June 10, 2013. Online. https://ssrn.com/abstract=2277117.

Carroll, Colleen. *The New Faithful: Why Young Adults Are Embracing Christian Orthodoxy.* Chicago: Loyola, 2002.

Casanova, José. "Rethinking Secularization: A Global Comparative Perspective." *The Hedgehog Review* 8 (2006) 7–23.

Cassidy, Laurie, and Maureen H. O'Connell, eds. *She Who Imagines: Feminist Theological Aesthetics.* Collegeville, MN: Liturgical, 2012.

Catechism of the Catholic Church. Vatican: Libreria Editrice Vaticana, 1997.

Cavalletti, Sophia. *The Religious Potential of the Child.* New York: Paulist, 1983.

Chi, Michelene T. H. "Three Types of Conceptual Change: Belief Revision, Mental Model Transformation, and Categorical Shift." In *International Handbook of Research on Conceptual Change*, edited by Stella Vosniadou, 61–82. New York: Routledge, 2008.

Chilton, Bruce. "Kingdom of God, Kingdom of Heaven." In *I–Ma*, edited by Katharine Doob Sakenfeld, 512–23. Vol. 3 of *The New Interpreter's Dictionary of the Bible.* Nashville: Abingdon, 2008.

Coffman, Pauline M. "Inclusive Language as a Means of Resisting Hegemony in Theological Education: A Phenomenology of Transformation and Empowerment of Persons in Adult Higher Education." PhD diss., Northern Illinois University, 1989.

Congregation for the Clergy. *General Directory for Catechesis.* Washington, DC: United States Conference of Catholic Bishops, 1998.

Conn, Walter. *Christian Conversion: A Developmental Interpretation of Autonomy and Surrender.* New York: Paulist, 1986.

Côte, Richard. *Lazarus! Come Out!: Why Faith Needs Imagination.* Ottawa, ON: Novalis, 2003.

Daily, Eileen. *Beyond the Written Word: Exploring Faith Through Christian Art.* Winona, MN: Saint Mary's, 2005.

Daloz Parks, Sharon. *Big Questions, Worthy Dreams: Mentoring Young Adults in Their Search for Meaning, Purpose, and Faith.* San Francisco: Jossey-Bass, 2000.

Damasio, Antonio R. *The Feeling of What Happens: Body and Emotion in the Making of Consciousness.* Orlando: Houghton Mifflin Harcourt, 1999.

Day, Dorothy. *The Long Loneliness.* New York: HarperOne, 1997.

Delbanco, Andrew. *The Real American Dream: A Meditation on Hope.* Cambridge, MA: Harvard University Press, 1999.

Dodd, Charles H. *The Parables of the Kingdom.* New York: Scribner, 1961.

Doran, Robert M. *Theology and the Dialectics of History.* Toronto: University of Toronto Press, 1990.

Dulles, Avery. *Models of Revelation.* Garden City, NY: Doubleday, 1983.

Durkheim, Émile. *The Division of Labor in Society.* New York: Free Press of Glencoe, 1964.

Dykstra, Craig. "Pastoral and Ecclesial Imagination." In *For Life Abundant: Practical Theology, Theological Education, and Christian Ministry,* edited by Dorothy C. Bass and Craig Dykstra, 41–61. Grand Rapids: Eerdmans, 2008.

Egan, Kieran, et al., eds. *Teaching and Learning Outside the Box: Inspiring Imagination Across the Curriculum.* New York: Teachers College Press, 2007.

Eisenstadt, Shmuel Noah. "Multiple Modernities." *Daedalus* 129 (2000) 1–29.

Eliade, Mircea. *The Sacred and the Profane: The Nature of Religion.* New York: Harcourt, 1987.

Erikson, Erik H. *Childhood and Society.* New York: Norton, 1963.

Eyler, Janet, et al. *Where's the Learning in Service-Learning.* 1st ed. San Francisco: Jossey-Bass, 1999.

Feuerstein, Reuven, et al. *Changing Minds and Brains: The Legacy of Reuven Feuerstein: Higher Thinking and Cognition Through Mediated Learning.* New York: Teachers College Press, 2015.

Fischer, Kathleen R. *The Inner Rainbow: The Imagination in Christian Life.* Mahwah, NJ: Paulist, 1983.

Foer, Joshua. *Moonwalking with Einstein: The Art and Science of Remembering Everything.* New York: Penguin, 2011.

Foster, Charles R. *From Generation to Generation: The Adaptive Challenge of Mainline Protestant Education in Forming Faith.* Eugene, OR: Cascade, 2012.

Fowler, James W. *Faithful Change: The Personal and Public Challenges of Postmodern Life.* Nashville: Abingdon, 1996.

———. *Stages of Faith: The Psychology of Human Development.* San Francisco: HarperSanFrancisco, 1995.

Francis I. "Evangelii Gaudium." Apostolic Exhortation, November 24, 2013. Online. http://w2.vatican.va/content/francesco/en/apost_exhortations/documents/papa-francesco_esortazione-ap_20131124_evangelii-gaudium.html.

———. "Gaudete and Exsultate." Apostolic Exhortation, March 19, 2018. Online. http://w2.vatican.va/content/francesco/en/apost_exhortations/documents/papa-francesco_esortazione-ap_20180319_gaudete-et-exsultate.html#The_logic_of_gift_and_of_the_cross.

Frankl, Viktor E. *Man's Search for Meaning.* Boston: Beacon, 2006.

Freire, Paulo. *Pedagogy of the Oppressed.* New Revised Twentieth-Anniversary ed. Translated by Myra Bergman Ramos. New York: Continuum, 1994.

Gallo, Carmine. "Thomas Jefferson, Steve Jobs, and the Rule of 3." *Forbes,* July 2, 2012. Online. https://www.forbes.com/sites/carminegallo/2012/07/02/thomas-jefferson-steve-jobs-and-the-rule-of-3/#131d6fee1962.

Garvey Berger, Jennifer. "Dancing on the Threshold of Meaning: Recognizing and Understanding the Growing Edge." *Journal of Transformative Education* 2 (2004) 336–51.

Geiger, Matthew. "Worldview Formation, Reflexivity, and Personhood: Their Essential Connectivity in Thick Perspective." *Religious Education* 112 (2017) 504–16.

Gilligan, Carol. *In a Different Voice.* Cambridge, MA: Harvard University Press, 1984.

Goto, Courtney T. *The Grace of Playing: Pedagogies for Leaning into God's New Creation*. Eugene, OR: Pickwick, 2016.

Greene, Maxine. "Realizing Literature's Emancipatory Potential." In *Fostering Critical Reflection in Adulthood: A Guide to Transformative and Emancipatory Learning*, edited by Jack Mezirow et al., 251–68. San Francisco: Jossey-Bass, 1990.

Groome, Thomas H. *Christian Religious Education: Sharing Our Story and Vision*. San Francisco: Harper & Row, 1980.

———. *Sharing Faith: A Comprehensive Approach to Religious Education and Pastoral Ministry: The Way of Shared Praxis*. San Francisco: Harper San Francisco, 1991.

———. *Will There Be Faith?: A New Vision for Educating and Growing Disciples*. New York: HarperCollins, 2011.

Haidt, Jonathan. *The Righteous Mind: Why Good People Are Divided by Religion and Politics*. New York: Vintage, 2012.

Harris, Dan. "Yael Shy: Helping College Students Fight Stress and FOMO." *10% Happier Podcast*, January 24, 2018. Episode 119. Online. https://www.yaelshy.com/features/2018/2/5/10-happier-with-dan-harris-ep-119-yael-shy-helping-college-students-fight-stress-and-fomo.

Harris, Maria. *Teaching and Religious Imagination*. San Francisco: Harper & Row, 1987.

Haughton, Rosemary. *The Transformation of Man: A Study of Conversion and Community*. Springfield, IL: Templegate, 1980.

Heinze-Fry, Jane A., and Joseph D. Novak, "Concept Mapping Brings Long-term Movement Toward Meaningful Learning." *Science Education* 74 (1990) 461–72.

Hess, Mary E. "Teaching and Learning Comparative Theology with Millennial Students." In *Comparative Theology in the Millennial Classroom: Hybrid Identities, Negotiated Boundaries*, edited by Mara Brecht and Reid B. Locklin. New York: Routledge, 2015.

Holstein, James A., and Jaber F. Gubrium. *The Self We Live By: Narrative Identity in a Postmodern World*. New York: Oxford University Press, 2000

hooks, bell. *Teaching Critical Thinking: Practical Wisdom*. New York: Routledge, 2009.

Ignatius of Loyola. *Constitutions of the Society of Jesus*. St. Louis: Institute of Jesuit Sources, 1996. Online. https://jesuitas.lat/uploads/the-constitutions-of-the-society-of-jesus-and-their-complementary-norms/Constitutions%20and%20Norms%20SJ%20ingls.pdf.

———. *The Spiritual Exercises and Selected Works*. Edited by George E. Ganss. New York: Paulist, 1991.

Imbelli, Robert P. *Rekindling the Christic Imagination: Theological Meditations for the New Evangelization*. Collegeville, MN: Liturgical, 2014.

Immordino-Yang, Mary Helen, and Antonio Damasio. "We Feel, Therefore We Learn: The Relevance of Affective and Social Neuroscience to Education." *Mind, Brain, and Education* 1 (2007) 3–10.

Isasi-Diaz, Ada Maria. "Kin-dom of God: A Mujerista Proposal." In *In Our Own Voices: Latino/a Renditions of Theology*, edited by Benjamin Valentin, 171–90. Maryknoll, NY: Orbis, 2010.

Jennings, Willie James. *The Christian Imagination: Theology and the Origins of Race*. New Haven, CT: Yale University Press, 2010.

Jeserich, Florian. "Can Sense of Coherence Be Modified by Religious/Spiritual Interventions?: A Critical Appraisal of Previous Research." *Interdisciplinary Journal of Research on Religion* 9 (2013) 1–36.

John of the Cross. "The Dark Night." In *John of the Cross: Selected Writings*, edited by Kieran Kavanaugh, 155–210. Classics of Western Spirituality. Mahwah, NJ: Paulist, 1987.

John Paul II. "Catechesi Tradendae: On Catechesis in Our Time." Apostolic Exhortation, October 16, 1979. Online. http://w2.vatican.va/content/john-paul-ii/en/apost_exhortations/documents/hf_jp-ii_exh_16101979_catechesi-tradendae.html.

———. "Redemptoris Missio: On the Permanent Validity of the Church's Missionary Mandate." Encyclical, December 7, 1990. Online. http://w2.vatican.va/content/john-paul-ii/en/encyclicals/documents/hf_jp-ii_enc_07121990_redemptoris-missio.html.

Johnson, Mark. *The Body in the Mind: The Bodily Basis Of Meaning, Imagination, and Reason*. Chicago: University of Chicago Press, 1987.

Joy, Vance. "Mess Is Mine." Track 2 on *Dream Your Life Away*. Audio recording. New York: Atlantic Records, 2014.

Keating, Thomas. *Open Mind, Open Heart: The Contemplative Dimension of the Gospel*. New York: Amity, 1986.

Kegan, Robert. *The Evolving Self: Problem and Process in Human Development*. Cambridge, MA: Harvard University Press, 1982.

———. *In Over Our Heads: The Mental Demands of Modern Life*. Cambridge, MA: Harvard University Press, 1994.

———. "What 'Form' Transforms?: A Constructive-Developmental Approach to Transformative Learning." In *Learning as Transformation: Critical Perspectives on a Theory in Progress*, edited by Jack Mezirow et al., 35–70. San Francisco: Jossey-Bass, 2000.

Kohlberg, Lawrence. *The Psychology of Moral Development: The Nature and Validity of Moral Stages*. San Francisco: Harper & Row, 1984.

Lakeland, Paul. *Postmodernity: Christian Identity in a Fragmented Age*. Minneapolis: Augsburg-Fortress, 1997.

———. *The Wounded Angel: Fiction and the Religious Imagination*. Collegeville, MN: Liturgical, 2017.

Langer, Ellen J. *The Power of Mindful Learning*. Boston: Da Capo, 1997.

Langer, Susanne K. *Philosophy in a New Key: A Study in the Symbolism of Reason, Rite, and Art*. 3rd ed. Cambridge, MA: Harvard University Press, 1957.

Levine, Amy-Jill. *Short Stories by Jesus: The Enigmatic Parables of a Controversial Rabbi*. New York: HarperOne, 2014.

Lewin, Tamar. "Record Level of Stress Found in College Freshmen." *New York Times*, January 26, 2011. Online. https://www.nytimes.com/2011/01/27/education/27colleges.html.

Lewis, C. S. *Mere Christianity*. New York: Macmillan, 1952.

Lichtmann, Maria. *The Teacher's Way: Teaching and the Contemplative Life*. Mahwah, NJ: Paulist, 2005.

Lipka, Michael. "Muslims and Islam: Key Findings in the US and Around the World." *Pew Research Center*, August 9, 2017. https://www.pewresearch.org/fact-tank/2017/08/09/muslims-and-islam-key-findings-in-the-u-s-and-around-the-world.

Loder, James E. *The Transforming Moment: Understanding Convictional Experiences*. San Francisco: Harper & Row, 1981.

Lonergan, Bernard. *Insight: A Study of Human Understanding. Collected Works of Bernard Lonergan.* Edited by Frederick E. Crowe and Robert M. Doran. Toronto: University of Toronto Press, 1992.

———. *Method in Theology.* Toronto: University of Toronto Press, 2007.

Lynch, William. *Images of Faith: An Exploration of the Ironic Imagination.* Notre Dame: University of Notre Dame Press, 1973.

Marr, Bernard. "How Much Data Do We Create Every Day? The Mind-Blowing Stats Everyone Should Read." *Forbes,* May 21, 2018. Online. https://www.forbes.com/sites/bernardmarr/2018/05/21/how-much-data-do-we-create-every-day-the-mind-blowing-stats-everyone-should-read/#270c4fac60ba.

Martin, James. *The Jesuit Guide to (Almost) Everything: A Spirituality for Real Life.* New York: HarperCollins, 2012.

———. *Jesus: A Pilgrimage.* New York: HarperOne, 2014.

Martinez, Michael E. *Learning and Cognition: The Design of the Mind.* Upper Saddle River, NJ: Merrill, 2009.

Marx, Karl. *Critique of Hegel's "Philosophy of Right."* Cambridge Studies in the History and Theory of Politics. Cambridge: Cambridge University Press, 1970.

McAdams, Dan. *The Redemptive Self: Stories Americans Live By.* New York: Oxford University Press, 2006.

McCarty, Robert J., and John M. Vitek. *Going, Going, Gone: The Dynamics of Disaffiliation in Young Catholics.* Winona, MN: Saint Mary's, 2017.

Merton, Thomas. "Learning to Live." In *Journey of Transformation,* edited by John Ranieri et al., 354–61. Plymouth, MI: Macmillan Learning, 2017.

———. *New Seeds of Contemplation.* New York: New Directions, 2007.

Mezirow, Jack. *Transformative Dimensions of Adult Learning.* San Francisco: Jossey-Bass, 1991.

Miller, Vincent J. *Consuming Religion: Christian Faith and Practice in a Consumer Culture.* New York: Continuum, 2004.

Moore, Karl. "Authenticity: The Way To The Millennial's Heart." *Forbes,* August 14, 2014. Online. https://www.forbes.com/sites/karlmoore/2014/08/14/authenticity-the-way-to-the-millennials-heart/#5da2d53a4531.

Morgan, Joyce H. "Displaced Homemaker Programs: The Transition from Homemaker to Independent Person." PhD diss., Teachers College at Columbia University, 1987.

Mulder, André, and Bas Van den Berg. *Learning for Life: An Imaginative Approach to Worldview Education in the Context of Diversity.* Eugene, OR: Wipf & Stock, 2019.

National Alliance on Mental Illness (NAMI). "Top Mental Health Challenges Facing College Students." *NAMI Northside Atlanta* (blog), July 31, 2015. Online. https://naminorthsideatlanta.org/college/top-mental-health-challenges-facing-college-students.

Naugle, David. *Worldview: The History of a Concept.* Grand Rapids: Eerdmans, 2002.

Newman, John Henry. *An Essay on the Development of Christian Doctrine.* Westminster, MD: Christian Classics, 1968.

Nhat Hahn, Thich, and Daniel Berrigan. *The Raft Is Not the Shore: Conversations Toward a Buddhist-Christian Awareness.* New York: Orbis, 2001.

O'Malley, Timothy. *Liturgy and the New Evangelization.* Collegeville, MN: Liturgical Press, 2014.

Ospino, Hosffman. *El Credo: Un Encuentro con la Fe de la Iglesia.* Notre Dame, IN: Ave Maria, 2017.

O'Toole, James M. *The Faithful: A History of Catholics in America*. Cambridge, MA: Belknap Press of Harvard University Press, 2008.

Ozment, Katherine. *Grace Without God: The Search for Meaning, Purpose, and Belonging in a Secular Age*. New York: HarperCollins, 2016.

Pariser, Eli. "Beware Online 'Filter Bubbles.'" *Ted Talks*, May 2, 2011. Video recording. Online. https://www.ted.com/talks/eli_pariser_beware_online_filter_bubbles.

Paul VI. "Dei Verbum." Dogmatic Constitution, November 18, 1965. Online. http://www.vatican.va/archive/hist_councils/ii_vatican_council/documents/vat-ii_const_19651118_dei-verbum_en.html.

———. "Evangelii Nuntiandi." Apostolic Exhortation, December 8, 1975. Online. http://w2.vatican.va/content/paul-vi/en/apost_exhortations/documents/hf_p-vi_exh_19751208_evangelii-nuntiandi.html.

———. "Gaudium et Spes." Pastoral Constitution, December 7, 1965. http://www.vatican.va/archive/hist_councils/ii_vatican_council/documents/vat-ii_const_19651207_gaudium-et-spes_en.html.

Perkins, Pheme. *Hearing the Parables of Jesus*. Mahwah, NJ: Paulist, 1981.

Peterson, Jordan. "Biblical Series I: Introduction to the Idea of God." Lecture delivered at Isabel Bader Theatre, Toronto, May 16, 2017. Youtube Video. 2:38:28. https://youtu.be/f-wWBG06a2w.

Pew Research Center. "America's Changing Religious Landscape." May 12, 2015. Online. https://www.pewforum.org/2015/05/12/americas-changing-religious-landscape.

———. "In US, Decline of Christianity Continues at Rapid Pace." October 17, 2019. Online. https://www.pewforum.org/2019/10/17/in-u-s-decline-of-christianity-continues-at-rapid-pace.

———. "Millennials in Adulthood: Detached from Institutions, Networked with Friends." March 7, 2014. Online. http://www.pewsocialtrends.org/2014/03/07/millennials-in-adulthood.

———. "'Nones' on the Rise: One-in-Five Adults Have No Religious Affiliation." October 9, 2012. Online. https://www.pewresearch.org/wp-content/uploads/sites/7/2012/10/NonesOnTheRise-full.pdf.

———. "A Portrait of Jewish Americans." October 1, 2013. Online. https://www.pewforum.org/2013/10/01/jewish-american-beliefs-attitudes-culture-survey.

———. "US Public Becoming Less Religious." November 3, 2015. Online. http://assets.pewresearch.org/wp-content/uploads/sites/11/2015/11/201.11.03_RLS_II_full_report.pdf.

Piaget, Jean, and Barbel Inhelder. *The Psychology of the Child*. Translated by Helen Weaver. New York: Basic, 2000.

Pitzele, Peter. *Scripture Windows: Towards a Practice of Bibliodrama*. Los Angeles: Torah Aura, 1998.

Polanyi, Michael. *The Tacit Dimension*. Chicago: University of Chicago Press, 1966.

Pollefeyt, Didier. "Difference Matters: A Hermeneutic-Communicative Concept of Didactics of Religion in a European Multi-Religious Context." *Journal of Religion Education* 6 (2008) 9–17.

Pramuk, Christopher. *The Artist Alive: Explorations in Music, Art, and Theology*. Winona, MN: Anselm Academic, 2019.

Pui-Lan, Kwok. *Postcolonial Imagination and Feminist Theology*. London: SCM, 2005.

Ratzinger, Joseph. *Faith and the Future*. San Francisco: Ignatius, 2009.

———. "Funeral Homily for Msgr. Luigi Giussani." *Communio* 31 (2004) 685–87. Online. https://www.communio-icr.com/articles/view/funeral-homily-for-msgr.-luigi-giussani.

———. *Truth and Tolerance: Christian Belief and World Religions.* San Francisco: Ignatius, 2004.

Regan, Jane E. *Where Two or More Are Gathered: Transforming the Parish Through Communities of Practice.* New York: Paulist, 2016.

Ricoeur, Paul. "Hermeneutics of Symbols and Philosophical Reflection." *International Philosophical Quarterly* 2 (1962) 191–218.

———. *History and Truth.* Translated by Charles A. Kelbley. Evanston: Northwestern University Press, 1965

———. *The Symbolism of Evil.* Translated by Emerson Buchanan. Boston: Beacon, 1969.

———. *Time and Narrative.* Vol. 1. Translated by Kathleen McLaughlin and David Pellauer. Chicago: University of Chicago Press, 1984.

Rolheiser, Ronald. *The Shattered Lantern: Rediscovering a Felt Presence of God.* Revised ed. New York: Crossroad, 2004.

Santiago, Briana. "Briana Santiago Synod Witness." *Young People, the Faith and Vocational Discernment* (blog), October 4, 2018. Online. http://www.synod.va/content/synod2018/en/youth-testimonies/witness-of-briana-santiago.html.

Schillebeeckx, Edward. *Christ the Sacrament of the Encounter With God.* New York: Sheed and Ward, 1963.

Schneiders, Sandra M. *Buying the Field: Catholic Religious Life in Mission to the World.* Mahwah: Paulist, 2013.

———. *The Revelatory Text: Interpreting the New Testament As Sacred Scripture.* 2nd ed. Collegeville, MN: Liturgical, 1999.

Sharot, Tali. *The Influential Mind: What the Brain Reveals About Our Power to Change Others.* New York: Henry Holt, 2017.

Small, Jenny L., ed. *Making Meaning: Embracing Spirituality, Faith, Religion, and Life Purpose in Student Affairs.* Sterling, VA: Stylus, 2015.

Smith, Christian. *Souls in Transition: The Religious and Spiritual Lives of Emerging Adults.* New York: Oxford University Press, 2009.

Smith, James K. A. *Desiring the Kingdom: Worship, Worldview, and Cultural Formation.* Grand Rapids: Baker Academic, 2009.

Starratt, Ruth S. "Education with a Sense of Wonder: A Spiritual Journey." *Journal of Catholic Education* 3 (1999) 8.

Sveinunggaard, Karen L. "Transformative Learning in Adulthood: A Socio-Contextual Perspective." In *35th Annual Adult Education Research Conference Proceedings*, edited by D. Flanner, 275–80. University Park: Pennsylvania State University, 1993.

Synod of Bishops (XIII Ordinary General Assembly). "The New Evangelization for the Transmission of the Christian Faith." Lineamenta, February 2, 2011. http://www.vatican.va/roman_curia/synod/documents/rc_synod_doc_20110202_lineamenta-xiii-assembly_en.html.

Taylor, Charles. *A Secular Age.* Cambridge, MA: Belknap Press of Harvard University, 2007.

Taylor, Edward W. "Analyzing Research on Transformative Learning Theory." In *Learning as Transformation: Critical Perspectives on a Theory in Progress*, edited by Jack Mezirow, 285–328. San Francisco: Jossey-Bass, 2000.

Tilley, Terrence W. *Faith: What It Is and What It Isn't.* Maryknoll, NY: Orbis, 2010.

Tracy, David. *The Analogical Imagination: Christian Theology and the Culture of Pluralism.* New York: Crossroad, 1981.

Twenge, Jean, et al. "Age, Period, and Cohort Trends in Mood Disorder and Suicide-Related Outcomes in a Nationally Representative Dataset, 2005–2017." *Journal of Abnormal Psychology* 128 (2019) 185–99.

United States Conference of Catholic Bishops. *Doctrinal Elements of a Curriculum Framework for the Development of Catechetical Materials for Young People of High School Age.* Washington, DC: United States Conference of Catholic Bishops, 2008.

Van der Kooij, Jacomijn C., et al. "'Worldview': The Meaning of the Concept and the Impact on Religious Education." *Religious Education* 108 (2013) 210–28.

Warnock, Mary. *Imagination.* Berkeley: University of California Press, 1976.

Weber, Max. *The Protestant Ethic and the Spirit of Capitalism.* New York: Scribner, 1948.

Wilson, Donna, and Marcus Conyers. *Teaching Students to Drive Their Brains.* Alexandria, VA: Association for Supervision & Curriculum Development, 2016.

Winner, Lauren F. *The Dangers of Christian Practice: On Wayward Gifts, Characteristic Damage, and Sin.* New Haven, CT: Yale University Press, 2018.

Wu, Tim. *The Attention Merchants: The Epic Scramble to Get Inside Our Heads.* New York: Vintage, 2017.